Simply Beautiful
Cakes

Jill Maytham

Published by Jem Publishers
PO Box 115, Kloof 3640
KwaZulu-Natal, South Africa
© Copyright 1997 Jem Publishers

ISBN 0-620-18921-5

Typeset, Layout, Design & Reproduction by Techno Decyan
Photography: Ivor Migdoll
Printed and bound by Interpak.

Foreword

It is with great pleasure I introduce you to this wonderful book, "Simply Beautiful Cakes". I have known Jill for many years and have had the privilege of teaching at her school in Pinetown, Natal, South Africa. Jill is full of enthusiasm for her craft and along with Neil, her very supportive husband, always coming up with innovative techniques and sugarcraft tools to help make the task of decorating a cake, or making decorations more quickly and with ease.

Sugarcraft and cake decorating have grown as a craft very quickly. Sometimes it is difficult to keep up with new trends and techniques. This book, however, is at the forefront of new ideas and methods and is aided by the beautiful layout with clear and concise step-by-step photographs and instructions. This is a must for any decorator or sugar artist.

I hope you will enjoy this book as much as I have and it will prove an invaluable source of information and ideas for all.

Nicholas Lodge

Nicholas Lodge
International Sugar Art Collection
Atlanta, Georgia USA

Preface

This book contains many new and creative ideas that are both easy to follow and simply explained. It is my hope that this book will stimulate the decorator's creative imagination when faced with the pleasurable task of creating cakes for special occasions.

This is not only an instruction book, but a collection of beautiful cakes lovingly created and dedicated to various people involved in my life.

I will be delighted if this book becomes a constant source of inspiration to the creative decorator, both novice and experienced alike.

Finally, brethren, whatsoever things are true, whatsoever things are honest, whatsoever things are just, whatsoever things are pure, whatsoever things are lovely, whatsoever things are of good report; if there be any virtue, and if there be any praise, think on these things.

Philippians 4 : 8

The Author

Jill Elaine Maytham

Jill's involvement in cake decorating began 24 years ago. Her natural talent and creative ability enabled her to quickly grasp the skills of this craft.

Her success exhibiting at shows and willingness to share her talents, resulted in Jill starting the first Branch of the South African Cake Decorators Guild in KwaZulu-Natal.

Identified as a leader in her field, Jill was chosen to be amongst the first group to enter the South African Cake Decorators' Guild Examinations for Teachers and Judges. These she passed with distinction. Her teaching abilities have been recognised throughout the cake decorating world.

Jill's desire to share her talents resulted in the writing of her first book "Sugar Flowers", first published ten years ago. The simple step-by-step instruction book has been reprinted five times enabling thousands to participate in this stimulating and creative hobby.

Over the years, Jill has collected many more ideas which she shares in her latest book "Simply Beautiful Cakes". Again, her easy-to-follow instructions will enable the cake decorator to enjoy producing something to bring pleasure to others.

The ongoing need for innovative equipment to assist cake decorators, led to the formation of JEM Cutters which Jill and her husband, Neil, own and run. JEM equipment may be found throughout the world wherever cake decorators gather.

Acknowledgements

I wish to record my indebtedness to Elsie Stapylton-Adkins who worked so hard with me in creating this book. As an expression of my thanks I have placed her name on the cover of this book. Elsie is a qualified cake decorating teacher and judge through the South African Cake Decorators' Guild. Elsie is responsible for the division of JEM Cutters where beautiful sugar flowers are manufactured.

I also thank my staff who helped us with the many repetitive tasks in the making of the decorations and flowers in this book. In particular I would like to acknowledge Lucy Nunnan, Vanessa Padyachee and Fathima Haroun.

Special thanks to Ivor Migdoll for the photography, to René Hartslief and Julia Ramsay from Techno Decyan for the typesetting, layout and repro. Thanks also to Patty Kearsey for proofreading the text.

Many others, too numerous to mention, who in any way helped this book reach finality, are also thanked.

Lastly, my special thanks to my husband Neil, for his love, patience and encouragement as I persevered with the creation of this second book.

It has been a privilege and honour to assist Jill in creating the decorations in her book "Simply Beautiful Cakes". I have learnt so much as we explored new techniques and ideas together. I am sure that the readers of this book will benefit as much as I have done.

Elsie Stapylton-Adkins

CONTENTS

CONTENTS

Butterfly

Butterflies may be made with or without the use of florist wire. The illustrations that follow, show the method without the use of wire. Should you wish to wire the butterflies, you could insert fine wire into the inside corners of the wings. Use a gauge 28 wire, taped with white florist tape that has been shredded into quarters. The JEM tape cutter is ideal for this purpose. Alternatively, a hooked wire could be placed into the body of the butterfly and the wings attached as indicated below.

Step 1

Lightly grease your worktop surface with Petal Base. It is essential that the paste is rolled out very thinly. It should be transparent. Cut out the wings and allow to dry flat. If you are using the wire method, you will need to cut out each wing separately, as you will need to roll out the paste allowing for the insertion of the wire.

When the wings are dry, lightly dust in the colours of your choice. Pale shades are recommended. The edges may be tipped in a slightly darker shade. Note that the centres have been left white.

Step 2

Using a soft paint brush, lightly apply a little lustre dust to the wings. A propelling pencil with a 0.35 lead was used to draw in the veins on the wings. To assist you in matching the opposite wing, it is recommended that you work on both of the opposite wings simultaneously. If you try to get too far ahead with painting one wing, you will find it is difficult to repeat the pattern evenly.

Note the layout of the wings in the cutter. This will assist you in assembling the butterfly. The large wings are attached to the top of the smaller wing. Place the larger wing over this and leave to dry. If you have used wire, tape the wings into this position.

HINT: For the best results, petals and leaves should be rolled out until they are almost transparent. Thick paste results in unattractive gum paste work.

Butterfly
... Continued

Step 3

Mix a small amount of dark brown paste for the body. Press this into the cavity found in the centre of the cutter, to form the body. Remove excess paste. You may like to make some markings on the body whilst it is in the mould. To insert the antenna, use a sharp instrument to make two little holes. Cut a fine black stamen in half and, using a little gum glue, insert the antenna in position. Use a sharp scalpel and make two slits on either side of the body for the insertion of the wings.

A fine hooked wire may be inserted into the body.
If you have wired the wings, tape them together when the body is dry.

Step 4

Place a little gum glue into the side incisions. Pick up both pairs of dry wings and gently ease into the soft body.

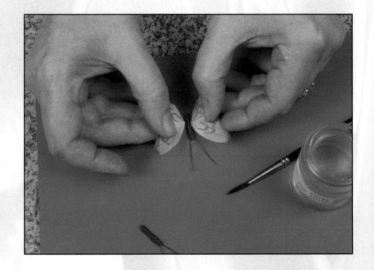

Step 5

Place the butterfly into a Handy Holder leg to support the wings until they are dry.

Butterfly

Butterflies made by Pam Milne of South Africa, using both sizes of JEM Butterfly Cutters.

Gardenia Wedding Cake

This cake was designed to fit onto an antique wedding cake stand. The three round cakes that were used for this cake measured 10" (25cm), 8" (20cm) and 6" (15cm) respectively. The cake boards were all exactly 1" (2cm) larger. The cakes were coated in the usual way. The boards were covered simultaneously in white sugarpaste. No shell border was used. Commercial silver bows have been used.

Step 1

Lightly grease your worktop surface with Petal Base. Roll out paste thinly and, using the middle sized rose petal cutter found in Set A10, cut out six individual petals. Place the petals on a Petal Pad and, using Tool 10, soften the edges of all the petals.

Step 2

Begin by making the centre of the flower. A taped wire gauge 20 was used for the flower. Place a tiny piece of flower paste on the end of the wire. Attach the individual petals, one at a time, using a little gum glue. Attach the petal to the stem and then allow each petal to curl backwards. The petals should slip into each other and should all be allowed to curl slightly backwards as each petal is added to the centre.

The centre of a flower that is past its best is also shown. Here the brown stamens are visible. Place a little paste on the end of your wire and make several tiny pieces of white paste stamens and attach to the centre. Shade these with a little yellow petal créme and lightly tip the ends with a touch of brown petal dust. Attach six of the same size petals as above, but this time do not curl the petals backwards but allow the formation to open up, creating a throat.

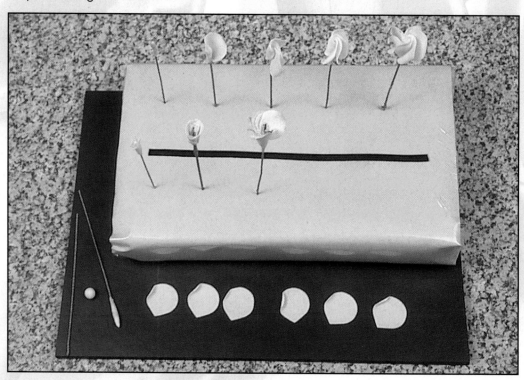

Gardenia Wedding Cake
... Continued

Step 3

Using Petal Base on your worktop surface, roll out thin white paste and cut out the next row of petals. Easy Rose Cutter No.60mm has been used. Place the petals on a Petal Pad and, using Tool 10, soften the edges. Curl some of the petals inwards and outwards using a cocktail stick. Place the wet petal on the back of petal former 3B and allow to partially dry. Attach to centre using gum glue. (See Step 7).

Step 4

Cut out one more petal using Easy Rose Cutter No.80mm. Work this petal in the same way. Tool 6 has been used on the larger petals. Petals should be holding their shape and then attached to previous row of petals. (See Step 7).

Step 5

Make a Mexican hat as illustrated. Roll out sufficient paste to fit over the 80mm cutter.

Gardenia Wedding Cake
... Continued

Step 6

Place the pointed hat over the centre of the 80mm cutter. Using your fingers, press paste against the edge of the cutter causing petals to be cut out. Work the petals on a Petal Pad in the same way as before, remembering to curl some petals inwards and others backwards. Slightly hollow out the centre as this forms the trumpet part of the flower.

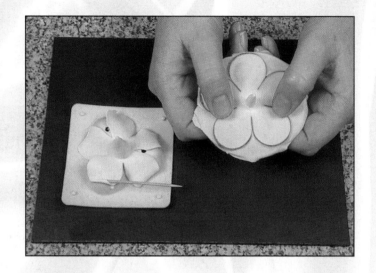

Step 7

Ease the final row of petals onto the back of the previous petals. Arrange petals carefully using a little sponge foam, and allow to dry.

Step 8

Make the calyx using green paste. Roll a small ball of paste slightly larger than a pea. Shape this into a teardrop. Using the six division side of Tool 9, ease this into the teardrop to make six divisions. A small pair of sharp scissors should be used to increase the length of the sepals. Pinch each section forming a ridge along the length of the outside of each sepal.

The calyx should be long and have a hollow centre as it will be required to cover the back of the flower, hiding the white trumpet.

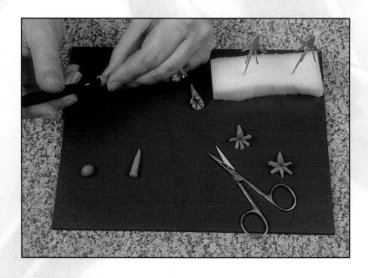

Gardenia Wedding Cake
... Continued

Step 9
Apply a little gum glue to the inside of the calyx and attach to the back of the gardenia.

Step 10
The leaves were made using several sizes of the water lily cutters found in set A8. The larger leaves were rolled out, not too thinly. Provision must also be made for the insertion of wire into the base of each leaf. The leaves were placed on a Petal Pad and were widened, using Tool 6. Smaller light green new leaves were made, as well as dark green mature leaves. These were taped together in clusters with the light green leaves at the tip of the stem. Brown florist tape should be used. The leaves were dusted appropriately and sprayed with a cooking spray to give them a sheen.

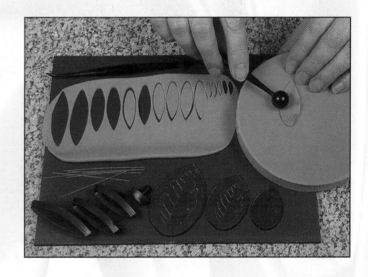

Step 11
A close-up of the gardenias.

Gardenia Wedding Cake
... Continued

Step 12

The trim on this cake was made using Strip No.5. A long length was rolled out on a lightly greased worktop surface. The strip was cut out about 1mm thick. Strip No.1 was pressed into the strip at intervals, creating a pattern in the centre of the band. The band was pinched at intervals and placed on the cakes. Gum glue was used to secure the band to the cake.

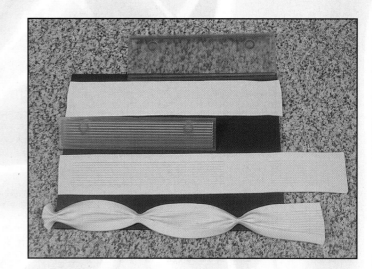

Instructions for making the drape bow appear on page 106.

Step 13

A close-up of the side of the cake.

Gardenia Wedding Cake

This cake is dedicated to Moe Vitcavich and Toni Hartman, my American friends, who have always been exceptionally kind to me on my many visits to I.C.E.S. in the U.S.A.

Crossword Puzzle Retirement Cake

A 12" (30cm) square tin was used for this cake and a 16" (40cm) cake board. The cake and board were covered together in cream sugarpaste (rolled fondant). Cream was mixed with a little egg yellow and a touch of malt brown, mixed into a small ball of paste. This was then added to sufficient plastic icing to cover the cake and board. The covered cake was left to dry for four days.

Work out your message on a piece of paper, bearing in mind that the message needs to be easy to read from the top and from left to right. Count out the number of white blocks you will need to contain the message. From this you will need to work out the number of black blocks you will require for your crossword puzzle. Once you have determined the number of squares needed, you will be able to measure the size of your crossword square to be placed on top of the cake. Using black paste, roll out a square the same size that the crossword puzzle is going to be. Place this in position on the cake, using a little water to secure. This will eliminate the possibility of any cream showing through the squares from the cake. Use a ruler as a guide when placing the blocks in position on the cake, to ensure the blocks are kept in a straight line.

Step 1

The blocks were cut out using the geometrical designs cutter No. A. When you have completed cutting out the blocks for the puzzle, cut out the message. Count out the required number of each letter contained in your message before you begin to cut out the letters. Remember for the best results the paste must not be too thin. Roll out the paste on a worktop surface that has been lightly greased with Petal Base.

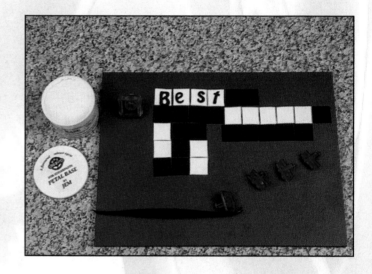

Step 2

To frame the puzzle, No.2 Strip Cutter has been used. This was cut long enough to cover the top of the cake and rest on the cake board.

The spiral around the base of the cake was made using the same strip cutter. This was evenly wound over the handle of a plastic spoon that had been lightly greased. As soon as the paste was holding the spiral, it was removed from the spoon and stretched out along the four sides of the cake. A little gum glue joined the spiral at each corner.

Crossword Puzzle Retirement Cake

... Continued

Step 3

The little rosette was made using one of the geometrical pattern cutters, No. J. These were simply folded in half to form a loop, using a little gum glue to secure. The loops were then placed in position, using a little gum glue.

Step 4

A close-up of the side of the cake

Pyracantha (Berries)

Step 5

These berries are found in a variety of colours, mainly red, orange and yellow.

Orange paste was used for the berries. Use a small amount of paste, slightly less than a pea, and roll your berries into shape. Using a pair of tweezers, pull out the centre of the berry to form the end of the core. Insert a fine hooked covered wire into the berry and leave to dry.

The dry berries were then shaded with Sunset Orange Petal Créme, Red Roses and Nut brown. The ends were dipped into a little brown pollen to emphasize the end of the core.

Crossword Puzzle Retirement Cake

... Continued

Step 6

The leaves were cut out in a dark green paste. Cutters No. B44, 45 and 46 were used, taken from Set B21. The leaves were cut out and the cutter moved down each leaf and cut a second time, causing smaller leaves to be cut out. Allow for wire insertion, (gauge 30, taped in green) when rolling out the paste for the leaves. The leaves were veined with veiners taken from Set V2. The leaves were dusted with a dark green petal dust and sprayed with a cooking spray to create a sheen. Allow the leaves to dry on a piece of paper towel.

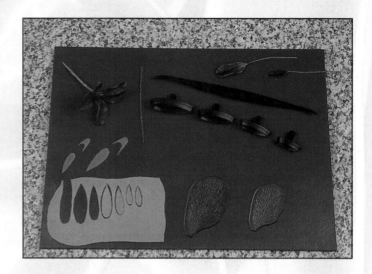

Step 7

Tape the berries in bunches of fives and sixes. Tape the leaves in a circle of five leaves, using several different sizes of leaves in each circle. Odd leaves do appear on the stem. Place a bunch of berries at the top of your stem and then proceed to add the leaves and berries at intervals.

Crossword Puzzle Retirement Cake

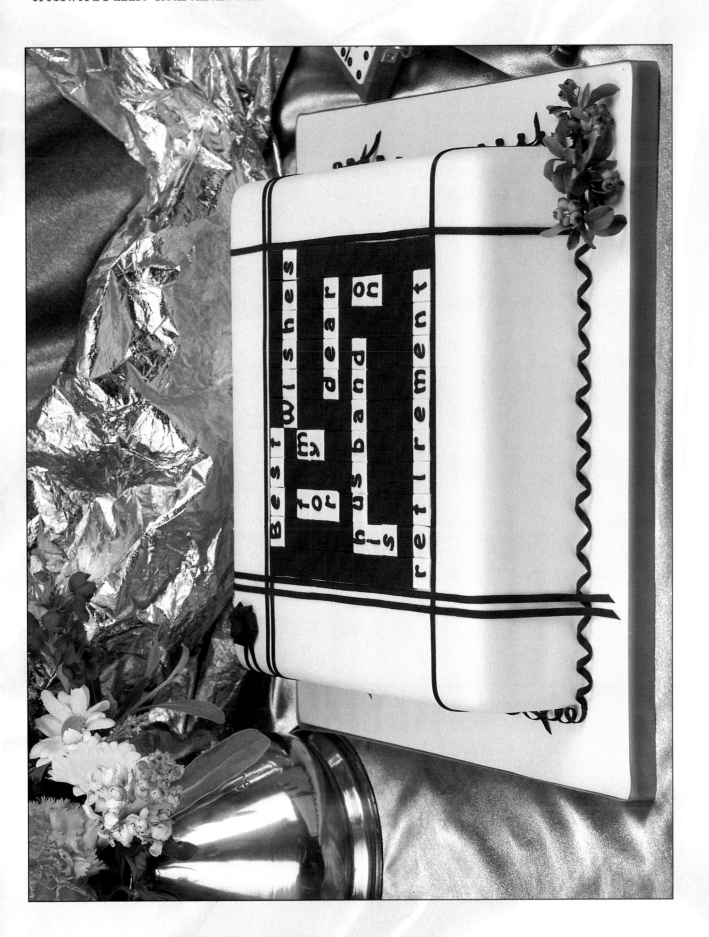

Crossword Puzzle Retirement Cake

This cake is dedicated to my beloved father, Murray McLachlan.

Bows

Several different sizes and types of bows have been made using two wide strip cutters: Strip 4 which cuts out two strips 23mm wide and Strip 5 which is 50mm wide. Bows could be used to go around the side of your cakes or form part of the decoration on the cake, for example on the corners, or they could be incorporated into your flower sprays.

Note: If you wish to lustre your bows, it is recommended that you apply lustre dust whilst the paste is still wet, using a large soft brush.

Step 1

Use Strip 5. Roll out a piece of paste long enough to form two loops joining in the centre of the paste. Alternatively, cut out two separate strips the length of the cutter for individual loops. Place a little duvet stuffing or foam into the loops and allow to partially dry. Use a dressmaker's wheel to make stitches on the edge of the ribbon.

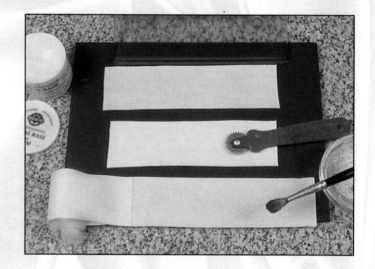

Step 2

Join the loops by squeezing them together in the middle. If you have made individual loops you will need to join them whilst they are still pliable. Use gum glue.

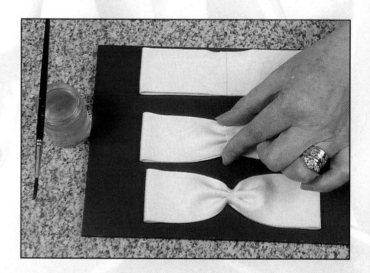

HINT: If you wish to colour sugarpaste (rolled fondant), break off a small ball about the size of a golf ball. Add the colour to this ball until the desired shade is achieved. Mix the coloured ball of paste into the sugarpaste. This will help avoid streaks. Remember that before covering your cake, the fondant should be 'worked' ensuring that it is soft and pliable, making it easy to cover the cake.

Bows
... Continued

Step 3

To make the knot to neaten the join, use Cutter No.J5-4 or cut an extra strip using Strip 5. Trim excess and fold the paste in a fan-like manner causing it to appear like gathered creases. Use gum glue to attach and neaten at the back of the bow.

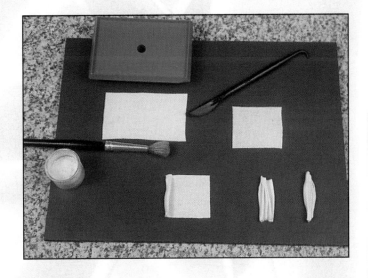

Step 4

Cut out a long strip to make the tails. Cut a 'V' into each end to neaten. Fold over as illustrated, allowing one tail to be longer than the other. Individual tails could also be used

Step 5

Make folds in the paste to create a soft material effect.

Bows

... Continued

Step 6

Using gum glue to secure, attach loops to the top of the tails. Leave to dry.

Step 7

Special effects may be made by using a plastic pot scourer to make impressions in the paste. Miniature Christmas cutters have also been used as embossers to add interest to the bow. Apply gold lustre to textured damp paste using your index finger.

Step 8

Textured bow.

Bows

... Continued

Step 9

Strip 4 has been used to make this multi-looped bow. Royal icing was stencilled onto the bow for a special effect. Cut out strips in various lengths. Bring the ends to the centre and place one loop on top of the next forming the multi-looped bow. Use a piece of the same strip cutter to neaten the knot. Use gum glue to secure the layers and the knot.

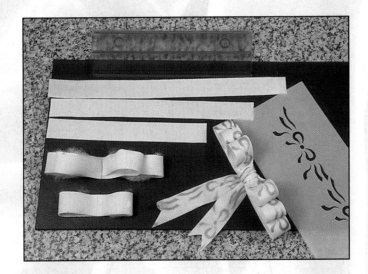

COVERING CAKES WITH ALMOND

Almond is used as a covering on fruit cakes to seal in the oils found in the fruit. If this is omitted it could result in the oils seeping through the sugarpaste (rolled fondant), causing your cake surface to be discoloured.

Before beginning, make sure that the cake is level.

1. Ensure that all the holes in the fruit cake are plugged with almond.

2. Place wax paper under the cake to keep the board clean.

3. Bring to the boil sufficient smooth apricot jam to cover the cake, mixed with a little water, to sterilize the jam. Cover the entire surface of the cake with the hot jam. Keep the cake board clean.

4. Roll out almond on sieved icing sugar. It should be about 5mm thick.

5. Lift up the almond either using 'lifters' - two panelite boards or a roller and place in position over the cake.

6. Smooth almond with a pair of JEM smoothers to eliminate any possible finger marks.

7. Rub a little extra icing sugar into the almond to strengthen and ensure that the cake is sealed.

8. Allow the almond to dry for at least 48 hours before covering with sugarpaste (rolled fondant).

Bows

Several ideas for bows.

Philippa's Christening Cake

A 12" (30cm) oval tin was used for this cake. The cake was coated in the usual way using pink sugarpaste (rolled fondant).

Step 1

Cut out the border next to the base of the cake, using a frill cutter F1A. This is an endless frill and you will be able to roll out paste in longer lengths than the cutter. Use a little water on the frill to attach to the cake and to the board.

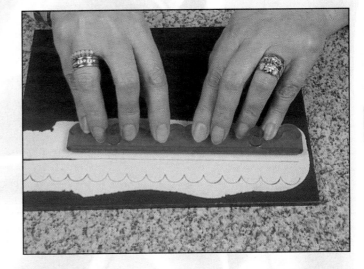

Step 2

Make a paper pattern to divide the cake into even scallops that fit around the cake. Measure the circumference of the cake. Fold the pattern in half, and in half again, until you have the desired number of even scallops. Using a pin, gently mark the outline of the scallops on the cake.

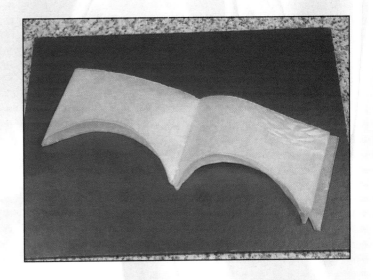

Step 3

Lightly grease your worktop surface with a little Petal Base and cut out sufficient pieces of Queen's Lace to attach to the scallops marked on the side of the cake. Remove the centres from the lace pieces before lifting the outer paste. This will prevent distortion of the soft paste. Dry thoroughly and attach to the cake by piping small neat dots of royal icing on to the outline of the scallop.

Philippa's Christening Cake

... Continued

The Cradle

Step 4

The cradle. Roll out some paste on a board lightly greased with Petal Base. The paste should not be too thin. Using cutter J5-4, cut out the base of the cradle. Place this over a roller and allow to dry completely.

Step 5

Cut out the headboard and the foot of the cradle, Set A21. Trim the foot of the cradle with an orchid cutter to add interest to the cradle.

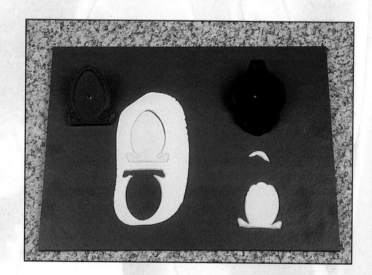

Step 6

Whilst the paste for the headboard and the foot of the cradle is still soft, press the dry base into either side of the cradle creating an impression of the curved base. Using the miniature heart cutter, make an impression in the headboard. Paint the hearts pink. When the headboard and the foot of the cradle are both thoroughly dry, assemble the cradle with a little royal icing.

Philippa's Christening Cake
... Continued

Step 7

To create an impression of a baby in the cradle, only the head will be seen. Mould a tiny head and a 'body' that will be placed under a blanket. Paint a little hair with a little petal dust mixed with a drop of alcohol. To make the pillow, roll out a piece of pink paste fairly thickly. Using the square cutter taken from the geometrical patterns, cut out a pillow. Trim, and using Tool 4A, lightly flute the edges.

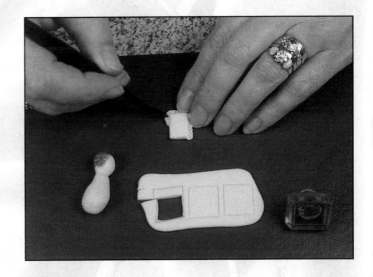

Step 8

The blanket has been woven using two strip cutters, No.1 and No.2. A combination of pink and white have been used to add interest to the blanket. Roll out paste in one colour and cut strips in it making sure to leave a border at the top. This will assist you in holding the weaving together.

Cut out separate strips in a different colour and a smaller strip cutter. Lift every second strip from the rolled out paste and, using a little water, attach the narrow strip into the weaving. Replace the strip and pick up the next strip. Continue doing this until you have sufficient paste woven to cut out your blanket for the cradle. Cut an extra strip for the edge of the blanket and lightly frill this using Tool 4A. Shape the wet blanket over the baby in the cradle.

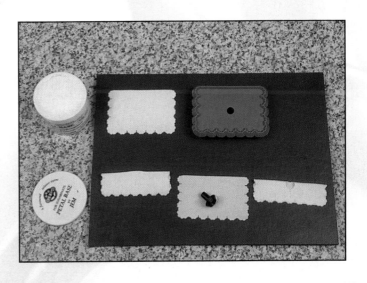

Baby's Dress
Step 9

Roll out paste thinly on a worktop surface, lightly greased with Petal Base. Using the small frilly card cutter, Set J5-11, cut out the top of the dress. Fold this in half to find the centre of the bodice, open up again and, using a small petal cutter taken from Set B19, cut out the neck.

Philippa's Christening Cake

... Continued

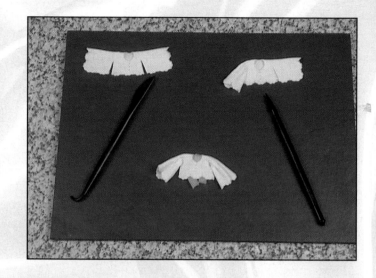

Step 10

Fold over again and now, using Tool 13A, make two incisions on either side of the neck to form the sleeves. Using Tool 16A, press in 'buttons' on the bodice. Place a tiny piece of sponge foam under the front of the bodice to give it shape.

Step 11

To make the skirt, roll out the paste thinly and using the same cutter, cut out a front and a back skirt. Fold in pleats. Attach skirt to bodice with a little gum glue. Lightly dust the dress with a little lustre.

Step 12

The finished dress

Philippa's Christening Cake

... Continued

Step 13

Cut out the name and whilst still soft, place on card J4-9 and leave to dry. Cut out two card supports, taken from Set J4-11. When dry, attach to card with a little royal icing.

Step 14

A close-up of the top of the cake (showing suggested layout).

Step 15

The side of the cake (showing detail).

Philippa's Christening Cake

This cake is dedicated to my niece, Philippa McLachlan.

Jasmine

Step 1

Place a minute amount of lime green paste on the end of a taped 28 gauge wire. This will become a tiny stamen found in the middle of a jasmine. Taper the paste on the end of the wire.

Roll a small amount of white paste into a ball about the size of a pea and then shape it into a tear drop. Flatten the outside edges and create a 'Mexican hat' effect. Using a small roller, thin the edges of the hat.

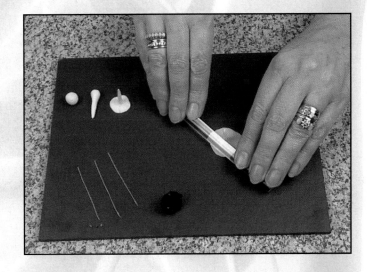

Step 2

Using the jasmine cutter, found in Set B16, place the 'Mexican hat' in the centre of the cutter and press your fingers on the cutter edge, causing the petals to be cut out.

Step 3

Place the trumpet of the cut out flower into a hole in the Mexican Petal Pad. Slightly open the throat of the flower using Tool 16A and then work each petal on the pad until they are thin, using Tool 10A.

Jasmine

... Continued

Step 4

Insert the wire through the centre of the flower. Allow the stamens to remain almost level with the petals. Use the 5 Petal Daisy Wheel cutter for the green calyx. Attach to flower with a little gum glue. Lightly dust the back of the flowers with a soft pinky mauve petal dust.

Step 5

Cut out a number of leaves, allowing for the insertion of wire. The top leaf is pointed and larger than the other leaves on the sprig. Use Cutter 63 taken from Set A14, and cutter B45 taken from Set B21, for the remaining leaves on the sprig. Dust with a darker petal dust. Spray with a cooking spray to give the leaves a sheen.

COVERING A DUMMY

1. Smooth away sharp edges with sandpaper.

2. Position dummy on cake board and secure. Office pins may be hammered through the back of the board and into the dummy. Alternatively, royal icing may be used to secure the dummy to the board. This should be allowed to dry before attempting to cover the cake with sugarpaste (rolled fondant).

3. Spread a little soft royal icing over the dummy to attach the sugarpaste.

Jasmine

A finished spray of jasmine.

This spray is dedicated to René Hartslief for her assistance and enthusiasm in compiling this book.

Christmas Tree Circle

A 10" (25cm) round cake and a 15" (38cm) cake board were used for this cake.
The cake and the board were covered in white sugarpaste (rolled fondant).

Step 1

A fairly dark green flower paste was mixed
for the Christmas trees. Lightly grease worktop
surface with Petal Base and cut out the
Christmas trees. Each of the eight trees on
top of the cake had four layers. Cut the top
three trees exactly in half and allow to dry.
Each tree needs one whole base.

Step 2

Begin assembling the 3-D trees on a flat base
tree. Pipe a line of green royal icing down
the centre. Place two halves in position. Pipe
another line of green royal icing. Proceed
until you have a total of eight halves on each
tree. Separate the halves with thin strips of
sponge foam and allow to dry. Cut out a red
miniature bow taken from the Miniature
Wedding set to decorate the trunk.

Step 3

The base frill was made using Endless Frill
Cutter No F2B. Roll out the paste on a lightly
greased surface about 1mm thick. Six
individual frills were cut out to go around the
circumference of the cake.

Christmas Tree Circle
... Continued

Step 4

Miniature Christmas trees were cut out to fit onto each frill. Red royal icing was piped on the edge of the frill using a No.3 nozzle. A dampened paint brush was used to flatten the edge to create a brush embroidery effect. The damp frills were attached to the cake, using a little water to secure.

Step 5

The gaps in the frills were neatened with the JEM Bow Size 3. The loops are brought into the centre of the paste and attached with a little gum glue. The knot is made from the little cut out piece in the cutter. The tails are joined to the top of the loops with a little gum glue. Attach bows with a little royal icing.

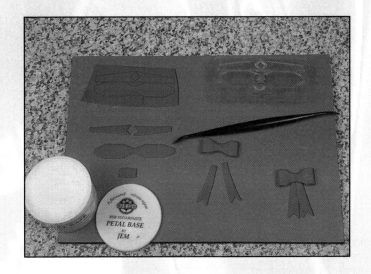

Step 6

A long red strip to neaten the top of the frill was cut out using Strip No.3. A little water was used to secure to the cake.

Christmas Tree Circle

... Continued

Step 7

A red and white disc was cut out for the centre of the cake. Cutter J4-15 was used to make the circles. The red circle shrunk slightly because there was insufficient icing sugar in the paste. This resulted in the white circle forming an edge.

Step 8

The JEM angels were cut out, taken from Set J6-13. The skirts were frilled with Tool 12A.

Step 9

Lustre the angels. Cut out the angels again and trim their wings. Using a little gum glue, attach the extra wings to the flat angels and leave to dry.

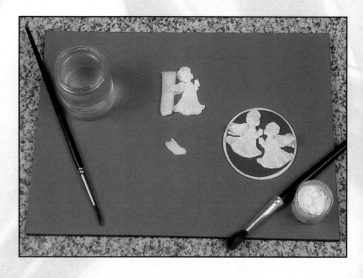

Christmas Tree Circle

... Continued

Step 10

A close-up of the side of the cake.

Step 11

The top of the cake.

HINT:

Keep cutters scrupulously clean.

Dirty cutters cause paste to stick in them.

Avoid storing metal and plastic cutters together.

Do not use a wet cutter.

When using extra large cutters, apply even pressure over the entire surface for a clean cut.

Christmas Tree Circle

This cake is dedicated to the late Adam Kearsey, whom I shall always remember leading the Kloof Methodist Choir into the church, singing "Once in Royal David's City ..." with his beautiful young voice. Adam was killed at the age of 9 whilst riding his bicycle. We will always remember you, Adam.

Yellow Rose of Texas

Three square cakes have been used for this cake. A 7" (18cm), 9" (23cm) and 12" (30cm) cake tin were used. The boards measured 8" (20cm), 11" (28cm) and 18" (45cm) respectively. The cakes and the boards were covered in white sugarpaste (rolled fondant) simultaneously. A shell border was piped at the base of each cake, using a No.7 nozzle.

The Garrett Frill

Step 1

A mixture of half sugarpaste and half flower paste has been used. The worktop surface was lightly greased with Petal Base. Roll out the paste about 2mm thick. The frill was cut out using the cutter in Set B9. Remove the centre. Frill the edges with Tool 12, using a backwards and forwards movement. Make an incision cutting the frill open, using Tool 13A.

Step 2

Measure the cake and work out how many scallops will fit around each tier. It is a good idea to make a paper pattern. The scallops used on this cake were made all the same size. This meant that two scallops were on the top cake, three on the middle tier and four were on the base cake. Attach the frills to the cake with a little water. When placing the frills together on the cake, be sure to hide the joins in the same manner as if you were working with material.

Pipe a snail's trail using royal icing on the top of the frill, using a No.1 nozzle. The scallops could have been cut out in different sizes by cutting out an even number of scallops from the frill. This would have enabled the decorator to have the same number of scallops on each tier, but in varying sizes.

Yellow Rose of Texas

... Continued

Step 3

A close-up of the roses and jasmine. Instructions to make these flowers may be found on page 111 and page 33.

HINT: For the best results, paste should be rolled out on a lightly greased surface. Use JEM Petal Base or white vegetable fat. This is not to be confused with white margarine. The vegetable fat found in the Petal Base retards the drying process of the paste, enabling you extra time to shape the petals before they dry. Avoid the use of cornflour. This tends to dry the paste and leaves a white residue, spoiling the effect of the petals. Cornflour (cornstarch) also clogs the cutters, causing the flower paste to stick in them.

Yellow Rose of Texas

This cake is dedicated to Elaine Garrett of South Africa, in acknowledgement of her idea in making the Garrett Frill which is used so frequently by cake decorators all over the world.

Azaleas for Shirley

Three round 6" (15cm) cakes were used to create a special effect. The cakes were covered with sugarpaste (rolled fondant) shaded mint green. A special cake board was made to support the three cakes and this board was covered separately with the mint green sugarpaste and allowed to dry for 2 days before the cakes were placed in position on the board.

Step 1

The JEM Double Heart side cutter was used for the sides. Lightly grease worktop surface with a little Petal Base. Roll out the paste evenly and cut out sufficient pieces to go around the three cakes. Place the double hearts over a box, or object, that has a right angle and leave to dry. A polystyrene ice cream box is shown in the photo.

Step 2

A small heart cutter taken from Set A20 was used to cut out green hearts to form a patten around the base of the cake and under each of the open hearts created by the side cutter. The green used, matched the leaves in the spray and was made using avocado green and black.

HINT: The use of a pair of smoothers is recommended to ensure no finger marks appear on the top and sides of the cake. If an air bubble should appear, insert a hat pin at an angle to release the air. Gently work the area with your fingers to remove the mark.

Azaleas for Shirley
... Continued

Step 3

Lightly grease your worktop surface with a little Petal Base and roll out green paste in a long strip. Using the endless strip cutter No.3 cut sufficient strips to edge the three cakes. Twist the strips between your fingers causing them to make a streamer. Place in position on the cakes. Attach to the cakes with a little water.

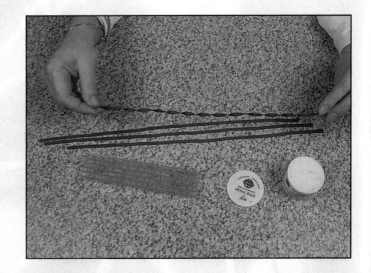

Step 4

Cut out a greeting card and the message. Cutter No.J5-1 was used.

Azaleas
Step 5

The pistil for the azalea was made using 26 gauge wire covered in white florist tape. Ten fine stamens were taped to the pistil in green tape that had been shredded into quarters using the JEM tape shredder. The ends of the stamens were tipped in a little burgundy paste colouring. A tiny piece of white paste was placed on the end of the pistil.

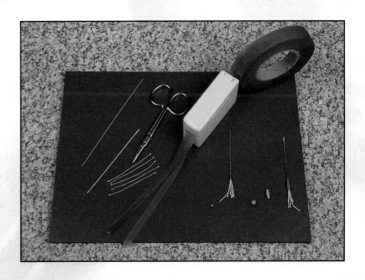

Azaleas for Shirley

... Continued

Step 6

Lightly grease your worktop surface with a little Petal Base. Form a small hump in the centre of the paste to strengthen the flower. Thinly roll out surrounding petals and, using Easy Rose Cutter 80mm, cut out the petals. Vein each petal with an orchid veiner taken from Set V4.

Step 7

Place petals on a Petal Pad and using Tool 10, lightly frill the edges. Slightly increase the size of one petal to form the central petal.

Step 8

Lift up one petal and place it in front of the one adjoining it to form the back petals. Note how the centre petal is lifted in front of the side petals.

Azaleas for Shirley
... Continued

Step 9

Place petals in flower former 4A and leave to dry in the Handy Holder. When the petals are dry, lightly dust the inside of the petals with a pale pink petal dust. The edge of the petals, both back and front, should remain white.

Step 10

The markings on both the two side petals and the centre petal, were made with a little burgundy dust mixed with a little alcohol. A cocktail stick was used to make the dots.

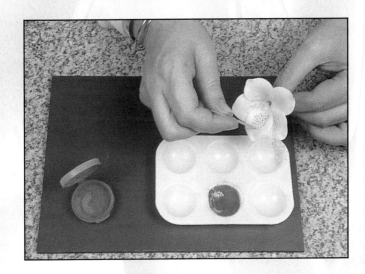

Step 11

The calyx was cut out using the sweet pea star calyx taken from Set B17. Roll out a small ball of paste and form a Mexican hat. Place the 'hat' over the cutter and press your fingers against the edges of the cutter to cut out the calyx. Use a little gum glue to attach to the back of the flower.

Azaleas for Shirley
... Continued

Step 12

Cut out numerous leaves using all the cutters in Set B21. Remember to work on a base lightly greased with Petal Base and when cutting out the leaves, allow for the insertion of wire at the base of the leaf. Vein the leaves using the hibiscus veiner Set V2.

Step 13

Place the leaves on a Petal Pad and lightly work the edges with Tool 10. Insert gauge 26 wire into the base of the leaves. Allow the leaves to dry. Dust them with a very dark green petal dust and spray them with a cooking spray to give them a sheen.

Step 14

Tape the leaves together using shredded tape. Begin with the smallest leaves. Tape the leaves in a circle using all the sizes until you have sufficient leaves for a sprig.

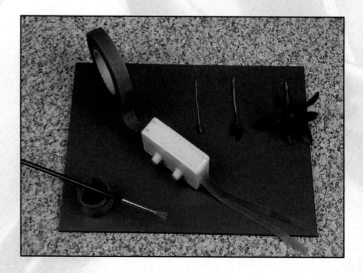

Azaleas for Shirley

... Continued

Step 15
The side of the cake.

Step 16
The azaleas.

This cake is dedicated to Shirley Crutchfield, my sister-in-law, whose courage I have always admired.

Prunus Blossom

Ready-made white JEM cotton centres have been used for the blossoms. To create the pollen effect, dip the tips of the stamens into some red Petal Créme. If you do not have ready made stamens, twist cotton around your finger about 12 times, and grip firmly with soft wire. Tape the stamens on to a 25 gauge wire. The buds were placed onto a gauge 25 green taped wire. A 30 gauge green taped wire was used for the leaves. The finished sprays were taped together with brown tape.

Step 1

Cutter No. B75 (set B15) was used for the petals. Lightly grease the board with Petal Base and roll out a little pale pink paste thinly. The Mexican hat method was used for the calyx, and a 5 Petal Daisy Wheel cutter. Using a tiny ball of green paste, smaller than a pea, roll the paste into a ball. Shape into a cone, and flatten the top to make a Mexican hat. Place this over one of the daisies in the 5 petal daisy wheel cutter. Using your fingers, press the paste against the cutter, causing the calyx of the blossom to be cut. *Using tool 4A, lightly flatten the sepals and open the calyx to support the petals.*

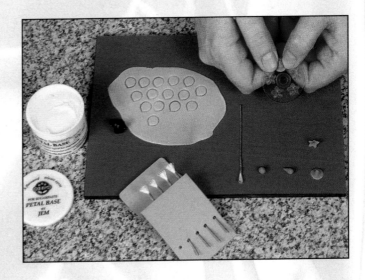

Step 2

You may now either insert the ready made stamens through the calyx and attach the petals individually, or you may place the petals on the calyx, using a little tylose glue to secure, and then pull the stamens through the centre of the calyx. Make sure your calyx is neat at the back of your flower. Allow blossom to dry in a Handy Holder, using Flower Former No.2B.

HINT: King and Queen's Lace Cutters. Paste should be rolled out thinly, but slightly thicker than paste recommended for petals and leaves. If paste is rolled out too thickly, it will stick in the cutters.

Prunus Blossom
... Continued

Step 3

The leaves were made from Set L10, using the two smaller cutters. The tiny leaves that appear on the end of the stems were made from a small cutter taken from Set B21. The paste was rolled out on a board lightly greased with Petal Base, with one side of the paste slightly thicker for the base of the leaf. This makes insertion of the taped wire easy.

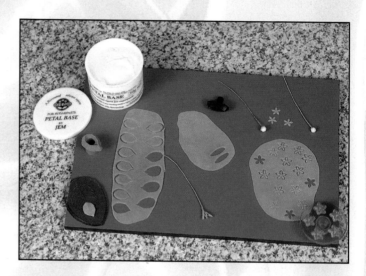

Step 4

The blossoms were dusted with a little pale pink petal dust.

The leaves were tipped with a little Burgundy petal dust, as they represent new leaves belonging to a Prunus. The Prunus will develop dark maroon leaves after the blossom has disappeared. The leaves were sprayed with a little cooking spray. This helps the petal dust to meld into itself and it also creates a natural sheen.

Step 5

Use brown tape to tape the blossom into a spray. A JEM tape cutter was used to cut the tape in half. When assembling blossoms, remember you will require several together with a number of blossoms in different stages of development. This adds interest and appeal to your exhibit. You will notice that very tiny closed buds have been used in the spray, together with slightly larger closed buds. Also incorporated in the spray are buds just about to open - in several stages. To add interest, one or two blossoms (that have lost petals) have been taped into the spray. In fact several calyxes without petals have been introduced into the spray. Dip the tips of the stamens into the red Petal Créme to create the impression of pollen. The twig effect in the taping of the spray is important, as this is how blossom grows.

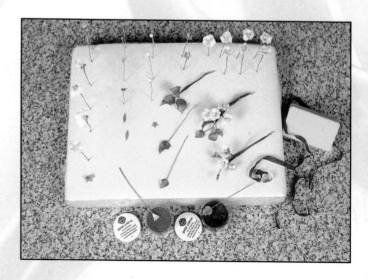

Prunus Blossom

... Continued

Step 6

When attaching the spray to the cake, use a little soft plastic icing the same colour as the cake. Dampen with a little water to make it sticky.

HINT: Lace pieces should be allowed to air dry before the centres of the lace are removed. This will prevent distortion. Lace pieces are generally used when they are dry.

Prunus Blossom

TAPE CUTTER
• The tape cutter is designed to shred tape into quarter widths.
• Blades may be removed by unscrewing the side of the tape cutter to adjust the width of the tape.
• Blades may be turned around when blunt.
• Make sure the blades are replaced evenly, or the cutter will not work properly. Before tightening the screws, lightly tap the tape cutter on a table to ensure the blades are level.
• Lift up the centre piece (shutter) - it is removable.

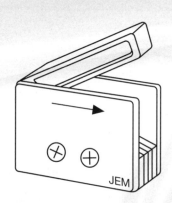

Left Hand

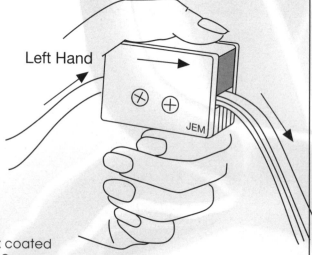

• Thread required length of florist tape with the wax coated side facing upwards, from behind the centre piece.
• Close the shutter.
• Apply gentle pressure to the centre piece and, using the other hand, pull the florist tape or tear ribbon through. Illustration shows tape cut in half and two quarter widths.

It's Christmas!

A flat-top diamond shape tin has been used. Cover the cake ahead of time in the usual way. Allow to dry for about one week. A board was made to order.

To achieve dark blue, mix Royal Blue and a little Jet Black into your sugarpaste (rolled fondant).

Step 1

Apply a little JEM Petal Base to the work board. Using the smallest 4 cutters in the JEM L5, poinsettia set, cut sufficient petals to create a baby poinsettia. Use JEM Tool 12, to vein the petals. Allow to dry.

Step 2

Make tiny stamens by forming a small tear drop in paste. Cut the tops to create stamens, using a small pair of scissors. Allow to dry. Roll bits of paste into the shape of a bean. Make two 'beans' and using Tylose glue, stick them together back to back. Immediately insert the dry poinsettia petals into the soft 'beans'. Try to avoid making the flower symmetrical.

HINT: Alphabet Cutters. Lettering should be cut out using sufficient paste to give the letters body. This means they should be rolled out thicker than paste recommended for petals and leaves. If paste is rolled out too thickly it will stick in the cutters.

Lettering should be allowed to air dry before the centres of the lettering are removed. This will prevent distortion. Lettering may be attached when it is still soft.

It's Christmas!

... Continued

Step 3

When the flower is set, tip the edges of the petals and leaves with gold dust that has been mixed with a little gin, or a little cocoa butter.

Step 4

Make a paper pattern to create an outline smaller than the top of your cake. Cut out sufficient strips to fit around the pattern. Three sizes of strips create an interesting border.

Cut strips carefully, making sure that both sides match before attempting to attach these to the cake. Place the strips back to back to check measurements.

Neaten any joins with a little icing.

Step 5

Cut out the Star JEM 6-2. You need one star for the base. Cut out an additional four stars. Cut these down the centre. Leave to dry. When dry, pipe a line of royal icing from the top of the star to the base using a No.2 icing nozzle. Place the first pair of star halves together in the centre of the base. In the same way attach the next 3 layers that form the star.

Beginning with the bottom layer carefully lift the sides of the star up. Insert small even strips of sponge foam between each layer. Work from side to side, until the star almost meets in the centre.

When the star is dry, tip the edges gold.

It's Christmas!

... Continued

Step 6

Cut out the window frieze to fit the sides of the cake. Leave to dry.
If you want to have the Miniature Christmas patterns in the windows, remove the window bars from the cut out.

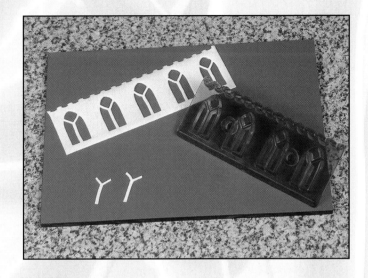

Step 7

Cut out strips using Strip No.3 the same length as the side of the cake and allow to dry. When dry, pipe a straight line of royal icing above the top of the windows and beneath the windows. Attach the dry strip No.3, standing on its side, and leave to set.

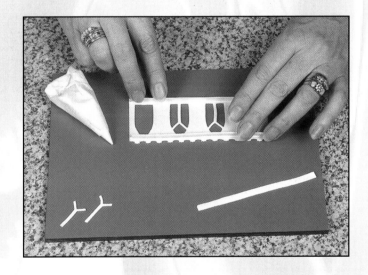

Step 8

Cut out miniature Christmas cutters of your choice.

It's Christmas!

... Continued

Step 9

Cut out the message using the JEM Alphabet Set. Dust with gold petal dust whilst still soft. Before cutting out the letters, the paste should be rolled out evenly and should not be too thick. Apply JEM Petal Base to the board for the best results. Lettering should remain on the board when cut out. Allow lettering to air dry before placing in position.

Step 10

Mix sufficient royal icing to pipe a shell border around the cake and a scroll on the board. You will also require royal icing to attach the frieze to the sides of the cake.

When piping a shell, remember that the nozzle should be almost touching the cake. Squeeze the icing bag, stop squeezing and pull the nozzle away from the shell, leaving a 'tail' on the shell. Begin piping the next shell on top of the tail.

Piping the scroll. Begin in the same way as the shell, but allow the icing to form a longer tail in the shape of an 's'. Pipe a 'c' leaning backwards into the back of the 's' tail. If you are unfamiliar with piping, it is recommended that you practice first.

In between using your piping bag, place the bag in your Handy Holder in the icing bag position. Dampen the sponge provided and this will keep your nozzle from drying out.

Step 11

Pipe royal icing on the strips attached to the sides of the window frieze. Attach to the cake sides. Hold for a few seconds to secure. The cake is standing on the JEM tilting turntable. A snail's trail could be piped against the cake to add strength to the frieze. Using a lightly dampened paint brush pick up the miniature cut outs and place them in position. Make sure that the frieze on all cake sides is level.

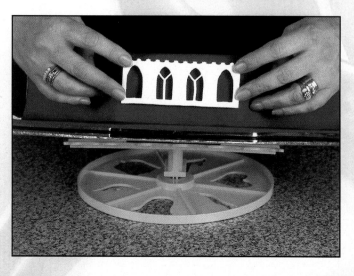

It's Christmas!

... Continued

Step 12

Neaten the join by lightly frilling a little piece of frieze from the wall. Use JEM Tool No.4A. Fold this in half, dampen the back of the paste slightly and ease into position.

COVERING THE EDGE OF A CAKE BOARD WITH RIBBON

Attach double sided sticky tape to the edge of the cake board. Remove the backing. Cut a length of ribbon using the backing (as a guideline for measurement) to go around the edge of the cake board. Attach ribbon to cake board.

If you have used tear ribbon, insert a pin level with the sugarpaste covering on the cake board surface. Draw the pin through the ribbon around the cake board.

If you wish to place a narrow ribbon on top of a wide ribbon, attach this to the wide ribbon **before** placing the wide ribbon on the cake board.

Place the double sided sticky tape on the cake board. Measure the amount of ribbon required.

Secure both ends of the wide ribbon in a straight line on a flat surface. (Use Prestik).

Place the narrow ribbon on the **edge** of the double sided tape. Cut off surplus tape.

Remove backing from narrow ribbon and place this in the centre of the wide ribbon whilst it is stretched out flat.

Attach the joined ribbons to the side of the cake .

Church

A mixture of half flower paste and half sugarpaste (rolled fondant) may be used to make the church. Roll out paste about 2mm thick. Half and half has been used in the illustrations. Pastillage may also be used. Pastillage would give you a more accurate effect and may be rolled out thinner. However, pastillage is very brittle.

Step 1

Mix two shades of light brown paste. Combine both shades but do not mix thoroughly. Lightly grease worktop surface with Petal Base and cut out two windows using the JEM Frieze Cutter No.1. Using strip No.1, make line impressions in the walls. Use Tool 13A to mark off 'bricks' in these lines. Leave to 'skin' dry before removing window pieces. Trim the panels to an equal size, each containing three windows. Allow panels to dry completely.

Step 2

Cut a paper pattern for the two ends of the church. Cutter J5-3 was used as a guide. Trim the top of the cutter to support the roof. Use a small nozzle to cut out a round window on the outside end of the church wall. Mark bricks into wall sides as indicated above..

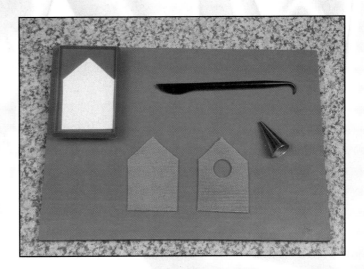

COVERING A SPONGE CAKE WITH SUGARPASTE (ROLLED FONDANT)
Bring to the boil sufficient smooth apricot jam to cover the cake, mixed with a little water. Paint the surface of the cake to prevent crumbs from being picked up into the sugarpaste. The almond covering is not necessary. Roll out sugarpaste (rolled fondant) in the usual way.

Church

Step 3

Cut out the turret tower using J4-7. Use the top of the Window frieze cutter to form the patterned edge. Cut out tower pieces exactly in half. Cut out a door, using the miniature bootee cutter. Do not remove inside as this forms part of the door. A window was created using a ribbon inserter tool as a guide.

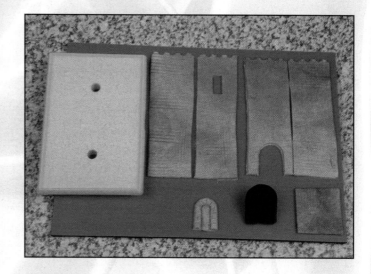

Step 4

Mix a little black and white paste. Combine both shades lightly so that an uneven effect is obtained when the paste is rolled out. Make a pattern for the roof that fits into Cutter J4-7. Cut out the roof using J4-7. Cut the roof in half using the pattern. Trim the edges of the roof with the edge of the Frieze cutter. Keep a piece in reserve as this will stand on top of the roof.

The clock face was made with white paste, using the base of an extra large nozzle as a cutter.

Step 5

Press the edge of the frieze cutter into the paste roof, creating markings that appear like roof tiles. Leave to dry.

Church

... Continued

Step 6

Sheet gelatine was used for the window panes. Strips to cover individual windows were cut up. Attach the individual strips to each window with a little piece of flower paste. A baby daisy cutter was used for this purpose.

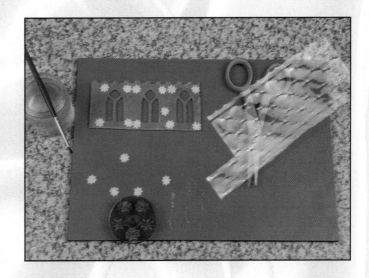

Step 7

To create a stained glass effect, a little red, blue and yellow petal dust were mixed with a drop of alcohol. A tiny flower was painted at the top of each window pane.

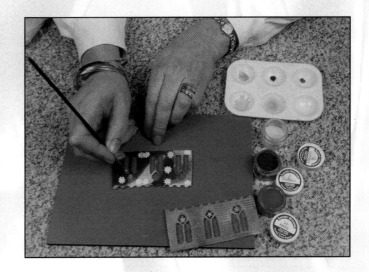

Step 8

Tiny pebbles were made to cover the board. Roll sufficient small balls of plastic icing in mottled shades of brown. The surface of the cake board was dampened. The pebbles were placed on the board. A little cornflour was dusted over the pebbles and they were flattened with a JEM smoother.

Church
... Continued

Step 9

The grass was made by pushing green paste through a sieve. This was left to dry. It was then applied to prepared areas on the pebbles that had been dampened slightly.

Step 10

To assemble the church, begin with the turret tower. A 5mm thick square of sugarpaste (rolled fondant) will assist in supporting the sides of the turret tower. Use the short sides of the turret tower to give you the required size. Royal icing, the same shade as the walls, was used to secure the base to the board. It was also used to join the sides of the tower of the church together. Use a No.3 nozzle.

Step 11

Cut out a platform of sugarpaste (rolled fondant) to support the church. Take the measurements from the end walls and the length of the window sides that have been cut out. Place the blank side of the church slightly recessed from the tower in position against the turret wall. Add the back window and the other end of the church.

Church

... Continued

Step 12

When the church pieces are all joined together, fill in gaps in the structure with a little royal icing.

Step 13

Place the roof in position. Pipe a line of royal icing on the apex and add the dry cut out edge, made from the pattern on the Frieze cutter. Use Tool 13 to press in steps in the sugarpaste, leading into the church.

Note: The cross shown on the outside wall of the church was made form a Cutter taken from Set A18.

Step 14

The 'earth' was made using cocoa powder and broken pieces of paste. The flowers were made from coloured pieces of broken paste.

Church

The Church is dedicated to my beloved husband, Neil, whose friendship I treasure.

Shirt for Denys

This cake was made in a Wilton rectangular shaped pan 13" (33cm) by 9" (23cm) that was 3" (8cm) deep. A cake board was made to order 16" (40cm) x 13" (33cm). The cake and the board were covered simultaneously in pale green sugarpaste (rolled fondant). This was allowed to dry for three days.

Step 1

A paper pattern was made for the tie. This was reduced in length. A pattern for the pocket and the collar were taken from a real shirt. The reinforcement that comes in the collar of a new shirt was used to support the shirt collar.

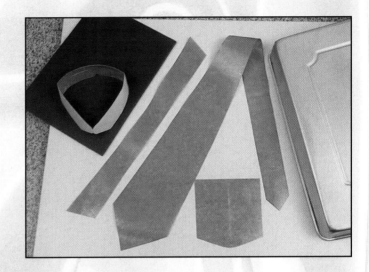

Step 2

Use half sugarpaste and half plastic icing for the collar in exactly the same colour as the base covering of the shirt. Lightly grease your worktop surface and cut out the collar. To avoid tearing the paste with a knife, use a pastry wheel to cut out the pattern. A dressmaker's wheel was used to make the stitches on the edge of the collar.

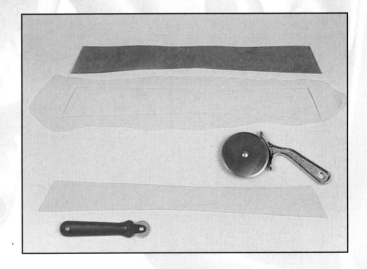

HINT: Lettering should be allowed to air dry before the centres of the lettering are removed. This will prevent distortion. Lettering may be attached when it is still soft.

Shirt for Denys
... Continued

Step 3
To obtain the correct shape, the collar was placed over the reinforcement that was found in a new shirt and allowed to dry.

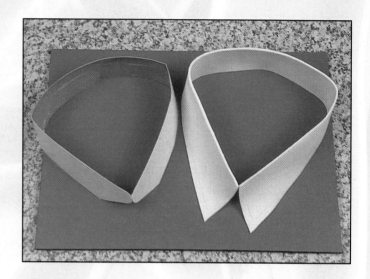

Step 4
The button band found in the centre of the shirt was cut out using Strip No.5. Strip No.2 was then pressed into this to create the effect of tucks. A dressmaker's wheel was used on the edges for added effect. Buttons were cut out using a small daisy centre stamp. These were evenly spaced on the band.

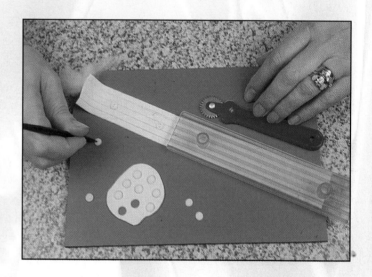

Step 5
Cut out a pocket. A narrow strip from strip No.2 was used to trim the pocket. The dressmaker's wheel added stitiches to the trim. A button was placed in the centre of the pocket.

Shirt for Denys

... Continued

Step 6

The size of the shirt represented Denys' age. The numerals were cut out using Set A1. The label was a cutter found in Set J5-6. This was placed on a contrasting background before being placed in position in the collar of the shirt.

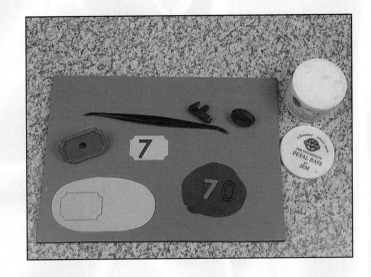

Step 7

The greeting cards were cut out using the cutter from Set J5-2. A hole was made in one corner of the card using the hole cutter that is found in Set J5-6. A narrow strip (No.1) was used to make the tag tie.

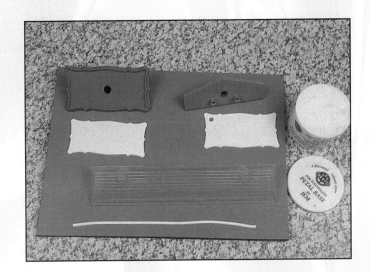

Step 8

Fold the strip in half. Thread the loop through the hole and pull the ends through the loop to grip the ribbon in the card. The name and message were cut out using the JEM Alphabet cutters.

Shirt for Denys
... Continued

Step 9
The geometrical Quilting Patch Designs were used to cut out various shapes and colours for the pattern on the tie.

Step 10
The tie was cut out using the pattern. A pastry wheel was used for this purpose. The patterns were placed in position by slightly dampening the reverse side with a little water. The tie was draped over the cake whilst it was still soft and allowed to dry.

HINT: You are working with food! Wash your hands before you begin, and frequently as you proceed.

Shirt for Denys

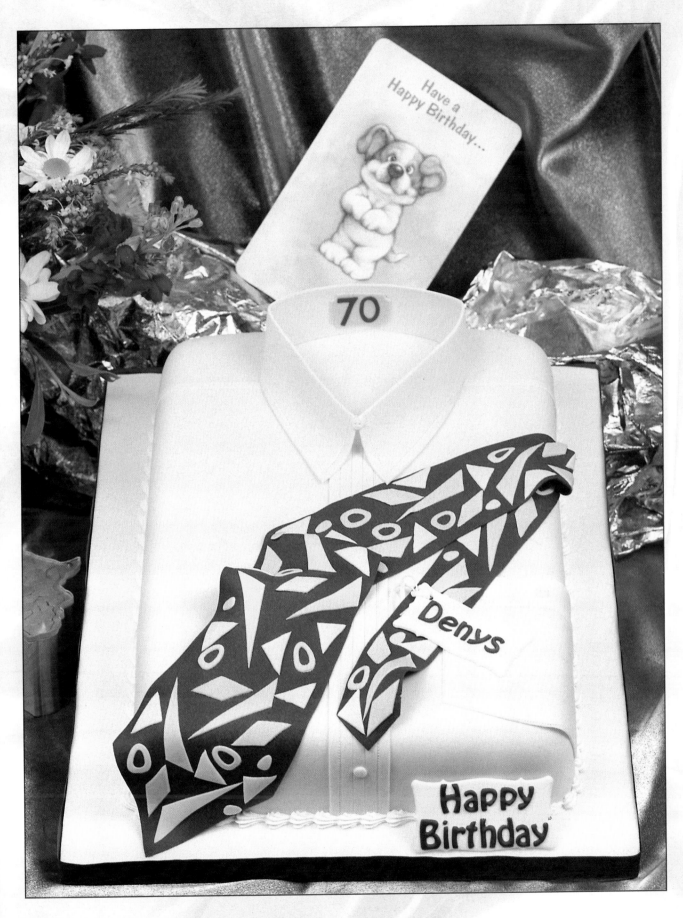

This cake is dedicated to Denys Stapylton-Adkins, Elsie's beloved husband.

Summer Wedding Cake

Three oval cake tins measuring 7" (18cm), 10" (25cm) and 12" (30cm) were used. The boards measured 9" (23cm), 12" (30cm) and 15" (38cm) respectively.

Cover the cakes in a cream sugarpaste (rolled fondant) in the usual way. Cover the cake boards at the same time. Pipe a shell border around the base of each cake.

Step 1

Using paste, cut out sufficient JEM Hollow Ovals and allow to dry over a curved surface. A used roll from tin foil or similar could be utilised for this purpose.

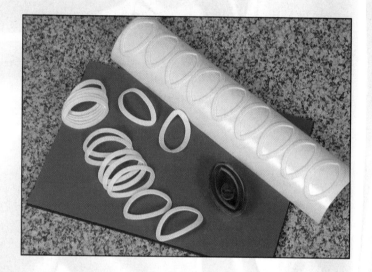

Step 2

Attach hollow ovals to the cake in the concave position with a little royal icing, leaving a small space between each oval. Finally place another oval in the convex position between the previous row of ovals.

HINT: Keep your flower paste sealed in a plastic bag placed in a plastic container with a lid. Each colour should be in a separate bag.

Summer Wedding Cake
... Continued

Sweet Pea
Step 3
Lightly grease your worktop surface with a little Petal Base. Roll out paste thinly. Cut out sweet pea using Set A5 and a middle size Rose Petal taken from Set A10. You will notice that the small arum lily cutter, Set A3, has been used to make an indent in the middle petal of the sweet pea. The petals should remain on the board after you have cut them out.

Step 4
Using JEM Tool No.4A, flute the edge of the centre rose petal. Attach this petal to a piece of taped wire to which a tiny piece of paste has been placed to give the centre petal body. When joining this petal to the wire, try to hide the centre without actually sealing the centre petal.

Flute the edges of the middle petal, using Tool 4A. Stroke the edge of the petal with the tool, lift the petal up and stroke it again. This movement will cause the petal to frill and slightly increase in size. (In a real flower, the middle petal is two single petals and is called the beak).

Step 5
Place a little gum glue at the base of the central petal and attach the middle petal. Allow the petals to hang forward. Leave to dry. When the centre petals are dry, cut out the back petal, known as the hood. Flute this petal, again using Tool 4A in the same way as described in step 3, *stretching the length of the petal slightly*. Attach to centre petals using a little gum glue at the base of the middle petal. *The back petal must stand away from the centre petals*. This is very important. A small piece of foam chip may be placed between the petals, separating them until they are dry.

Cut out the calyx, attach to dry flower by placing a little gum glue in the centre of the calyx. Allow sepals to curl downwards.

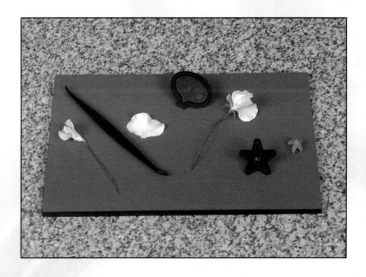

Summer Wedding Cake
... Continued

Step 6

When completely dry, shade your sweetpeas using the Petal Créme. A brush with a flat base should be used. When shading your sweetpeas, remember that the centre of this flower is usually paler than the outside petals. Petal dust could also be used.

Note: Remember when taping sweetpeas together, keep the same colour together on each stem.

Instructions on making roses appear on page 111.

Glossary of Terms

SUGARPASTE, PLASTIC ICING, ROLLED FONDANT, REGAL ICE and PETTINICE.
The above is a collection of names used in various parts of the world, all given to the silky smooth covering that is used to cover the cakes illustrated in this book.

FLOWER PASTE, GUM PASTE, MODELLING PASTE, PASTE
The above are names given to the pliable paste used for the making of sugar flowers and decorations for cake decorating.

PETAL CRÉME
A fragrant créme formulated to give sugar flowers subtle shading with the suggestion of a sheen. It is best applied to soft petals, using your fingers. Petal Créme is excellent on roses. If applied to dry petals, a firm flat paint brush is recommended.

Petal Créme may also be mixed with a little icing sugar and used on small stencils. It may also be used to decorate chocolates.

GUM GLUE, TYLOSE GLUE
Mix 5ml Tylose C1000p in 200ml water. Allow the tylose to dissolve. 5ml icing sugar may be added to this.

PETAL BASE
A specially formulated release agent, with a fragrance, for cake decorating.

Summer Wedding Cake

Confirmation Cake

A 12" (30cm) Oval cake tin was used for this cake. The cake was covered in the usual way using pale lemon sugarpaste (rolled fondant). The cake board was a 16" (40cm) oval.

Step 1

The JEM Frieze Cutter No.1 Window was used for the side of this cake. Lightly grease your worktop surface with Petal Base and roll out your flower paste evenly and not too thinly. Cut out six individual window strips for a cake this size. Trim the sides neatly.

Lightly grease the tin you have used with Petal Base and place the window frieze over each end of the tin. Place two window pieces on the front and back of the sides of the tin and allow to dry completely. When they are dry they will be able to stand.

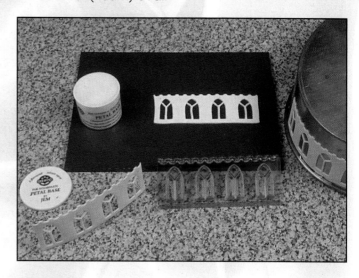

Step 2

Take a small handful of plastic icing and shape into the 'pages' of the Bible. Make sure that this will fit into the card cutter you will use for the cover of the book. Neaten and score with No.1 strip cutter to create the effect of multiple pages.
Cut out the back of the book using the card back cutter, Set J4-7.
To create a 'leather' look, a piece of plastic shower glass was used to emboss the cover of the Bible.

Step 3

Cut out a front cover still using J4-7, emboss to create a leather look, and then press the cross into the flower paste, leaving the impression of the cross (J6-14). Carefully paint the cross impression gold. The gold dust was mixed with a few drops of gin and painted on to the cover. Cut out the spine of the book using the same cutter. Trim and join the back of the book to the front cover. Use gum glue to secure. Using the Medium strip No.2, neaten the join of the spine to the top of the book. Short strips were cut, painted gold and placed at right angles to the joining strip. See Bible on cake.

Confirmation Cake

... Continued

Step 4

Make a book-mark, cutting out a wider strip in cream coloured flower paste. Use Strip No.4 (not illustratred). Allow this strip to be longer than the length of the book. Press Strip Cutter No.1 into the end of the bookmark to create a fringe. Using the Christian fish cutter, also found in Set J6-14, press it into the book-mark. Paint fish and fringe gold.

Cut out a champagne glass to make a chalice - Set J6-17. This was decorated by pressing Daisy Point Tool No.16A into the flower paste creating a pattern. Paint gold.

Step 5

Tiny baby ivy leaves were cut out. The back of the leaves was left slightly thicker than the tips of the leaves, and fine taped wire (gauge 30) was inserted into the leaves. The leaves were veined with V3. A small piece of sponge foam was used tor an even impression of the veining. The leaves were taped together in groups of between 7 and 9 leaves and placed in between the window friezes around the cake board.

Step 6

The window frieze pieces were attached to the cake with a little royal icing and allowed to dry.

Confirmation Cake

This cake is dedicated to my many friends in South Africa and all over the world, who share my love for, and faith in, the Lord Jesus Christ.

Eucharis Grandiflora

Also known as the Amazon Lily. The name Eucharis is taken from Eucharist meaning Lord's Supper.

Step 1

You will need two wires taped together for the pistil. A white taped gauge 30 wire is joined to a 20 gauge wire taped in green. Use the Handy Holder and the flower former to support the finished flower, to measure the combined length of these wires. The white wire will be the pistil and the green wire the stem. Make a tiny little head for the pistil, about the size of a pin, that is divided into 3 segments.

Step 2

Make the cup-like trumpet. Begin with a ball of paste about the size of a marble. Use Tool 2B to begin opening the ball to form the cup. Switch to Tool 5A to widen the top of the cup.

Step 3

At this stage, transfer the cup into the top of the handle on the Cutter from set B3. This is an excellent guide for creating the correct size of the cup. Use your fingers to ease the paste against the inside of the cutter.

Eucharis Grandiflora
... Continued

Step 4

Use the double edged side of Tool 5B and mark the inside of the cup dividing it into six segments. Make the first mark and then make the second mark exactly opposite it. Now carefully make the next two double vein marks in each segment, creating a total of six double veins in the cup.

Step 5

Using the back of the freesia cutter, Set B34, press into the top of the cup to make a scalloped impression in between the double vein marks. This will effectively create longer pieces of paste at intervals. Use a pair of scissors to trim the surplus long bits in between what will become the six stamens.

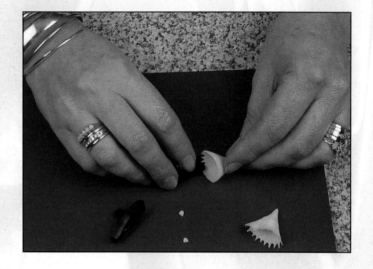

Step 6

Using a pair of tweezers, pinch the six bits of paste to create thin stamens that stand higher than the remaining top of the cup. These stamens should be coloured a very pale green/grey - they have a whitish appearance.

Eucharis Grandiflora

... Continued

Step 7

Note: Place your cup-like trumpet into a small plastic bag to prevent drying out whilst you work on the next step.

To make the lateral petals for the Eucharis lily, you will need a ball of paste the size of one and a half marbles. Following the principles of making a Mexican hat, roll the paste out evenly around the point of the hat.

Step 8

The paste should be rolled thinly and it should be rolled out until it is large enough for Cutter B3 to fit over it.
Place the Mexican hat in the centre of the cutter and cut one row of lateral sepals. Place the petal on a Petal Pad, and lightly ball the edges of the petal.

Step 9

Turn the paste over and vein with a Corn leaf veiner. (Set V5). Begin to hollow out the point in the hat. Use the same tools as for the cup-like trumpet to achieve this.
Note: This trumpet should have a fairly long pointed tail to it.

Eucharis Grandiflora

... Continued

Step 10

Using a Mexican Petal Pad, and Tool 4A, slightly frill the edges. Work the tool over the edge of the petals pulling down gently on the inside of the petals to slightly cup the side of the petals. *Using Tool 5B, mark in a double vein down the centre of each petal.* Place petals onto a Flower Former 5A that has had the centre cut out with a pair of scissors, approximately the size of a marble. The pointed part of the lateral sepal trumpet will fit into this. Clip into a Handy Holder. *To make sure you will be able to attach the pistil and the cup to the lateral sepals, insert an 18 gauge wire through the long trumpet in the lateral sepals creating a small passage way. The wire of the pistil attached to the cup will have to pass through it. (Remove the 18 gauge wire).*

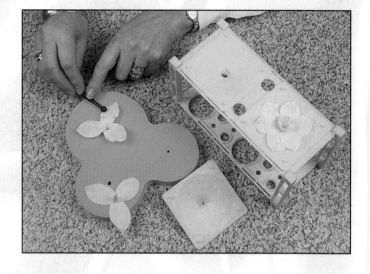

Step 11

Cut out the remaining 3 petals using Cutter No.B65 (the iris cutter). Working on a petal pad with a ball tool, Tool 10B, slightly increase the length of these petals.

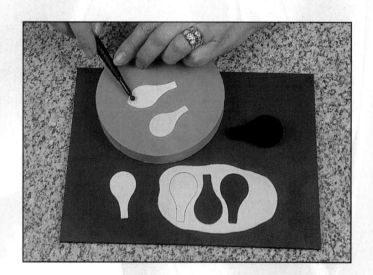

Step 12

Vein with the corn leaf veiner (V5), work these petals in the same way as the other lateral sepals, forming soft edges and a slight fold in the petals. Vein with Tool 5B.

Eucharis Grandiflora
... Continued

Step 13

Assemble the individual petals between the lateral sepals by placing a little gum glue in the throat of the flower.

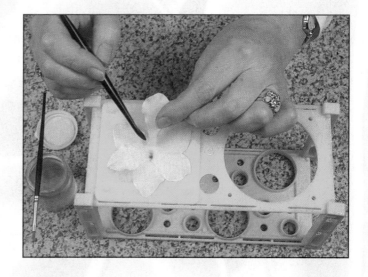

Step 14

Gently ease the prepared pistil into position in the cup-like trumpet of the flower. Finally, place the cup you have prepared and coloured, into the sepals. *Use Tool 10A and B to secure.* Gently ease the pistil into position through the opening created by the 18 gauge wire.

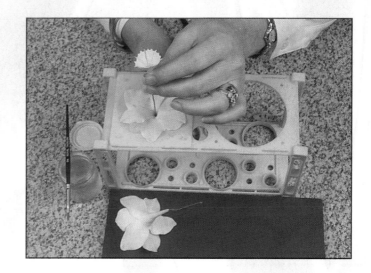

Step 15

When the flower is dry, carefully shade the double veins inside the cup-like trumpet a pale lime green. A touch of lime green can be placed on the outside of the cup slightly below the top of the cup. Petal Créme was mixed for this purpose, more yellow than green.

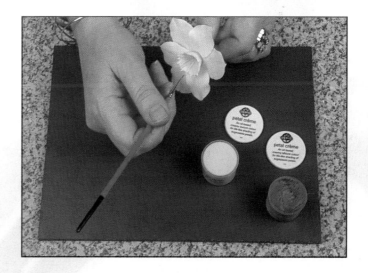

Eucharis Grandiflora

... Continued

Step 16

Lightly dust the petals with a little lustre dust, mixed with cornflour. This will give the petals a light sheen.

Step 17

To make the leaves, roll out green paste, creating a vein down the centre of the paste for the insertion of taped wire. Using the anthurium cutter, Set B22, cut out a number of leaves.

Step 18

Place the leaf on a petal pad, mark in veins using Tool No.4B. Lightly ball the edges with a ball tool. Dust with a darker shade of petal dust, and spray leaves with a cooking spray to give them a sheen.

Eucharis Grandiflora

Eucharis Grandiflora

This spray is dedicated to Patty Kearsey in appreciation of her assistance with proofreading this book.

Acorns and Oak Leaves

A 9" (23cm) round tin was used for this cake. The cake board was 13" (33cm). The fondant icing was shaded with a malt brown. Cover the cake and the board simultaneously.

Step 1

The card may be made from flower paste or pastillage. Flower paste was used in this instance. Lightly grease your worktop surface with Petal Base and roll out the paste, not too thinly. To create a 3-D greeting card, three sides were cut out using Cutter J4-7. The centre of the middle card was removed by using Cutter J4-9. Ensure the card edges are not distorted. Allow to dry completely.

Step 2

To assemble the card, roll out a little fondant about 1cm thick. The dry card sides should be used as a guide to cut out a triangle to form a supporting base for the cards. Use Tool 13 to cut the fondant.

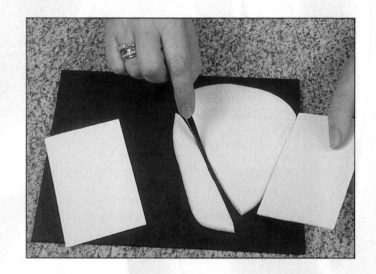

Step 3

Secure the dry cards to the soft base with a little royal icing. Remove any excess icing with a paint brush. Leave to dry.

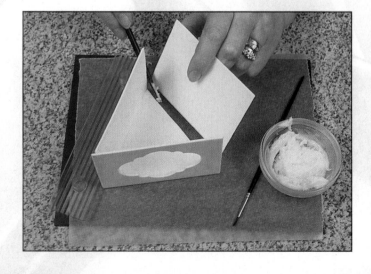

Acorns and Oak Leaves

... Continued

Step 4

To create the frill at the base of the cake, Cutter F5 was used. Measure the circumference of the cake. Lightly grease your worktop surface with Petal Base. Roll out a paste sausage and then using your roller, roll out the paste to about 1mm thick. Cut a single strip to fit around the base of the cake.

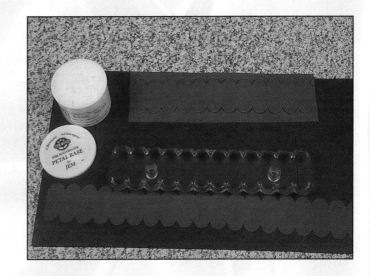

Step 5

Using a soft beige coloured royal icing suitable for piping loops and a No.2 nozzle, pipe several loops in the scallops of the frill. Use a damp paint brush to soften the loops into the frill. Remove any excess water on the brush before attempting the brush embroidery. When you have completed the required length of frill, position it evenly against the base of the cake. The frill should be attached to the cake while still damp.

Step 6

The message was cut out in a contrasting shade. Cover message with a little cling wrap or other suitable object, to prevent it from drying out. The ribbon was measured against the message and cut out using Strip No.4. Cut out a "V" on the edges of the ribbon. Attach the message to the ribbon while still damp. You may need to use a damp paint brush to secure the lettering to the ribbon. The ribbon was placed on the side of the cake and allowed to fall into place naturally. The ends were slightly dampened with a little water to secure.

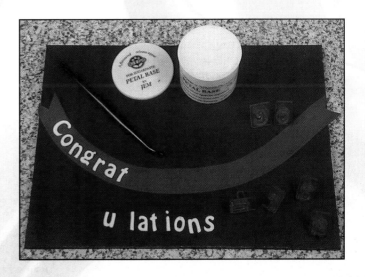

Acorns and Oak Leaves

... Continued

Acorns and Leaves

Step 7

Shade sufficient paste using malt and nut brown and a little avocado green. Roll a small ball of paste, slightly smaller than a marble, into an oval shape suitable for the acorn. A small hook was made on a 20 gauge wire taped in green. This was inserted into the acorn. Pinch the top of the acorn with a pair of tweezers.

Step 8

To form the cup for the acorn, a darker shade of paste was mixed by adding a little black to the paste. A Daisy Centre Stamp, large enough to hold the acorn, was used. The paste was placed over the stamp and Tool No.10B was used to hollow out the cup. The impressions from the stamp form the outside of the cup. Use a little water or gum glue to secure.

Step 9

Using a beige coloured paste, cut out the required number of oak leaves in a variety of sizes using Set L3A. When rolling out the paste remember to lightly grease the board with Petal Base and to allow for the insertion of wire at the base of each leaf by creating a small ridge for the wire. Vein the leaves using Set V1.

Acorns and Oak Leaves
... Continued

Step 10
Place the leaves on a Petal Pad and using Tool 10, lightly "ball" the edges to create a softened effect.

Step 11
Shade the leaves using a variety of petal dusts. Ochre, yellow, olive green and a touch of red dust were used. Place the leaves and the acorns on a piece of paper towel and spray with a cooking spray to create a sheen. Allow to dry before taping into a spray.

Step 12
Gently ease the spray through the cavity in the card and position it on the cake.

Acorns and Oak Leaves

This cake is dedicated to my younger brother, Dennis McLachlan, who has always been a special friend to me.

Cosmos Wedding Cake

A two tier cake was made for this cake. A 10" (25cm) square tin was used for the large cake and a 7" (18cm) cake tin for the smaller cake. The cakes were placed on boards 15" (38cm) and 9" (23cm) respectively. A 7" (18cm) square cake board was used to support the flowers creating a three tier effect.

The cakes and the cake boards were covered simultaneously. The extra board was also covered in pink sugarpaste (rolled fondant).

Cosmos comes in a variety of colours. The colours used to make the different shades were rose pink, white, magenta. A mixture of mauve, deep pink and a touch of royal blue was combined to make the deep burgundy shade.

Step 1

A very full centre is required for this flower. To save time, three ready made JEM cotton centres have been used. These have been dipped into yellow petal créme to give the stamens body. If you wish to make your own centres, follow the instructions on page 192.

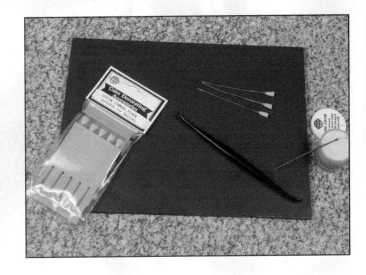

Step 2

Cut eight black stamens in half, making a total of at least sixteen black stamens. These should be taped evenly around the three cotton centres. Use a pin or a sharp instrument to separate the cotton stamens. Dip the cotton tips into yellow pollen.

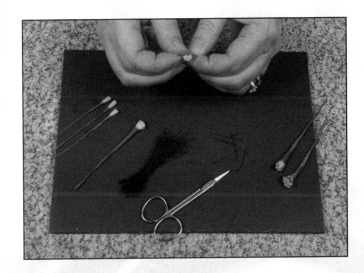

HINT: Only use authentic non-toxic food colouring to colour flower paste.

Cosmos Wedding Cake

... Continued

Step 3

Lightly grease your worktop surface with Petal Base. Roll out paste thinly and, using the Cosmos Cutter, cut out two rows of petals.

Step 4

Work petals on your worktop surface using Tool 12A. Roll tool backwards and forwards until the petals are thin and very well fluted. The cosmos has eight single petals. Place one layer of four petals over a second layer.

Step 5

Lift up two of the petals from the bottom layer and allow them to rest on top of the second layer of petals.

Cosmos Wedding Cake

... Continued

Step 6

Place petals in flower formers 1A for large flowers and 2A for half open flowers. Using a paint brush, apply a little gum glue to the base of the cotton stamens. Ease the stamens into position through the centre of the petals. To add movement, small pieces of sponge foam could be used to lift some of the petals. Allow to dry.

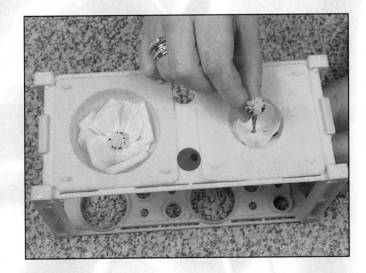

Step 7

The cosmos flower has a double calyx. To make the first calyx, use the Mexican hat method. Roll a little paste into a ball about the size of a pea. Flatten the edges creating the peak for the hat. Use a small roller to extend the perimeter of the flattened paste. Lift up hat and place the peak over the middle of the cutter. Press thumbs against the cutting edge causing the calyx to be cut out. Use tool 2B to slightly open the inside of the calyx. Attach to the back of the flower with a little gum glue.

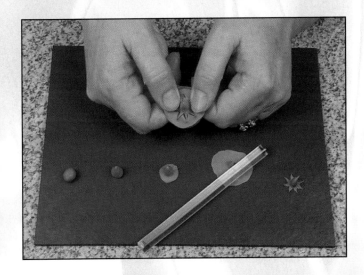

Step 8

Roll out the second calyx flat on a lightly greased surface. Place the calyx on a Petal Pad and using Tool 10, flatten the sepals of the calyx. Use a little gum glue to attach the second calyx to the back of the cosmos. Ensure that this calyx stands away from the first one.

Cosmos Wedding Cake

... Continued

Step 9

Buds are made in green paste using one of the middle sizes of the Daisy Centre Stamps. Press paste into stamp. Mark in eight divisions using Tool 13A to represent the developing petals. Attach a calyx to the buds. Dust buds with petal dust appropriate shade.

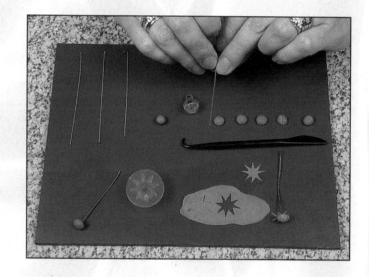

Step 10

Leaves were made from florist tape shredded into quarters with the JEM Florist Tape Cutter. The tape was twisted to form individual leaves and was taped onto a 26 gauge central wire.

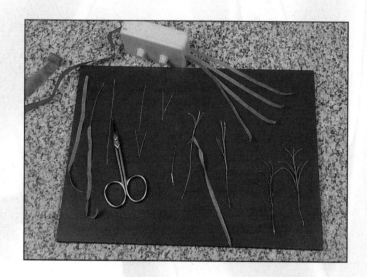

Step 11

Tape a few buds and leaves to each flower stem, using shredded florist tape.

Cosmos Wedding Cake

... Continued

Step 12

A close-up of the cosmos.

Step 13

A wire coat hanger was used to support the flowers. The hanger was taped in florist tape and then bent around a cylinder shape similar to the one in the illustration.

Step 14

To give the wire ballast, a thick piece of sugarpaste (rolled fondant) was cut out using a scone cutter.

Cosmos Wedding Cake

... Continued

Step 15

The wire frame on to which the flowers are to be taped.
Begin taping flowers on to the firm wire at the top of the frame, working towards the base.

Step 16

Kings lace has been used to decorate the sides of the cake. The cake sides were measured. A pattern was made. A row of royal icing dots was piped onto the pattern outline. The lace pieces were placed into position. For instructions on cutting out lace, see page 183.

Cosmos Wedding Cake

Cosmos wedding cake. This cake is dedicated to Margie Smuts, the founder of the South African Cake Decorators' Guild in appreciation of what she did for this art form in South Africa and abroad.

Phantom of the Opera

An 8" (20cm) cake tin was used for this cake. The cake was placed on a 10" (25cm) cake board. The cake was covered in sugarpaste (rolled fondant) shaded grey. The cake was positioned at the back of a 16" (40cm) cake board to add interest to the display. The cake and the small board were covered simultaneously. Allow covering to dry for at least 48 hours before any work is attempted. Black and white have been used exclusively on this cake. Instructions for the orchid may be found on page 146.

Step 1

Lightly grease worktop surface with Petal Base. Roll out black and white paste separately and cut out geometrical designs to create the pattern in the centre of the cake. Cutters taken from the Quilting Patch Designs are J and D. Allow patterns to air dry before moving them. This will prevent distortion. Work out pattern on cake top. Cut out sufficient patterns using Cutter J for the hollow shapes on the top of the cake and allow them to dry completely.

Step 2

Assemble the dry hollow shapes. Alternate between having a black and white base and black and white tops. Royal icing and Strip No.2 were used on the inside to join the patterns together. Make sure joins are neat. Leave to dry. Black and white pieces should be cut out using Cutter J to form the band around the centre of the cake and the circumference of the larger board.

It is easier to position patterns when they have air dried for a short while but while they are still soft.

HINT: If dry petals have a rough edge, use an emery board to neaten finish.

Phantom of the Opera
... Continued

Step 3

A close up of the pattern on top of the cake. The middle was made using Cutter. J. The top of the diamond shapes have been covered with a long black strip using Strip No.2 to neaten the join. This strip is long enough to rest on the extra large cake board creating a streamer effect.

Step 4

Cut out the face masks in black and white using Cutter J5-15. Small single daisy petal cutters may be used to cut out the eyes. The smallest cutter in Set B21 was used for the eyes. The mouth was made by pressing in half the end of a small plastic roller. Ease the mouth open. The masks may be happy or sad. Make a tiny hole on either side for the ribbon. The No.4 icing nozzle could be used. Shape over a curved object, eg. a small jar or a roller and allow to dry.

Step 5

Cut out trimmings from daisy leaves. Cutters from Set L4B and L6B are illustrated. Strip No.1 was used for the masks' ribbon. Decoration could be attached to the flat mask or a mask drying over a cylinder shape. Use a little gum glue.

Phantom of the Opera

... Continued

Step 6

The decorated masks in black and white with the ribbon threaded through the holes.

Step 7

A mask made using a pair of angel/swan wing cutters taken from Set J5-14. These were cut out in black. Eyes were cut out using a small narrow cutter. The masks were joined together with gum glue. The edges of the mask were painted with silver dust that had been mixed with a little alcohol. Strip No.1 was used to make the handle for the mask. This was plaited to give it both strength and interest. Allow the mask to dry over a glass jar that has been covered with wax paper. The small snowdrop cutter taken from Set B16 is also illustrated.

HINT: There are several ways to make the same flower. Find the simplest method to suit yourself.

Phantom of the Opera

This cake is dedicated to my mother, Joan McLachlan, who has given me many happy memories and an appreciation of good theatre.

Emily's 21st Birthday Cake

A large, open book cake pan made by Wilton, was used to bake this rich fruit cake.

The cake board was a piece of board cut to size. To raise the cake board slightly, two smaller square cake boards were placed under the hard board, creating an inner border measuring about 5 cm. The cake board was covered separately in pink and allowed to dry for three or four days. The edge of the cake board was covered with a scalloped ribbon to blend in with the colours in the cake and to hide the cake boards under the main board. Double sided tape was used to attach the ribbon to the board. Cover the cake with marzipan in the usual way. Allow at least 24 hours before covering the cake in sugarpaste (rolled fondant) coloured cream.

To colour the sugarpaste cream, mix a little egg yellow and malt brown into a small piece of sugarpaste, about the size of a golf ball. Add the small coloured ball to the necessary amount to cover the cake. Avoid adding colouring directly into sugarpaste - it is harder to mix through and may cause streaks in the covering.

Step 1

Place the rolled fondant over the book shape, smooth and neaten with the use of a pair of Smoothers, then use a large ball tool to create an indentation in the spine of the book and on either side of the book at the top and the base. Lift up the cake carefully and place on the dry covered cake board. *Two pieces of panelite board were used to lift the cake on to the board.*

To make the outer cover for the book, measure the sides of the book. Roll out a long sausage of Burgundy coloured paste, flatten and cut out a strip. Work on one half of the book and then the other. Use something to texture the outside cover to create a leather effect (wall paper was used). Use a ruler to push against the cover of the book to create a straight edge. Neaten with a pastry wheel. Lightly dampen the board immediately next to the book and under the Burgundy border to ensure the cover is stuck down.

HINT: The use of a pair of smoothers is recommended to ensure no finger marks appear on the top and sides of the cake. If an air bubble should appear, insert a hat pin at an angle to release the air. Gently work the area with your fingers to remove the mark.

Emily's 21st Birthday Cake

... Continued

Step 2

To create the effect of a number of pages on the side of the cake, measure the outside of the one half of the book, from the back spine to the front spine, and roll out a piece of gum paste as wide as the side of the book. Using the narrow strip cutter, No.1, make indentations in the icing to look like pages, keeping the 'pages' as straight as possible. Make as many impressions as you think it needs. Be careful not to cut the paste. Using a bit of water on a paint brush, brush the sides of the cake, and place the strip 'pages' in position over the one side of the cake. Repeat for the other half of the book. Trim where necessary.

Loose pages. Cut out a paper pattern to the page size required. Roll out gum paste using Petal Base to ensure the pages are easy to lift up. Cut out several loose pages for the book. A ruler and a pastry wheel were used to cut the pages. Avoid using a knife, as this tends to tear the pages. Leave pages where you have rolled them out, allowing them to 'skin dry'. This will eliminate the possibility of distorting the pages when you attempt to lift them into position.

Step 3

Work out your message. Count the number of individual letters you will need for the message and cut them out together. When cutting out lettering, the paste should not be too thin. If it is too thick, it will stick in the cutters. Keep the cutters scrupulously clean, remember to roll out the paste on Petal Base, or a white vegetable fat to avoid sticking. A little Petal Base could be rubbed over the paste before you cut out the letters. The lettering was shaded with Old Gold petal dust, whilst they were still soft. A little water was used to attach them to the pages. To keep the lettering in a straight line, make a pattern using a piece of folded wax paper, this will assist you in placing the letters on the pages.

Cut out a 21st key - (Set J5-13) to add an extra dimension to the content of the page. The numerals 21 were taken from (Set A1) to complete the message.

Attach the pages with a little water, or gum glue, to the centre of the book.

Remember to allow some movement in the pages - especially at the top of the cake. *This will create the impression that the pages actually turn.*

Emily's 21st Birthday Cake

... Continued

Step 4

Roll out a long strip of paste to make the book-mark. Using white royal icing, and a small fine stencil, create a pattern on the book-mark. Use a small piece of sponge to wipe the stencilled area after each application. This will eliminate any uneven ridge that could remain after stencilling. The fine strip cutter, No.1 was used to cut a fringe into the base of the book-mark. Lightly lustre the book-mark to create a satin effect. When placing the book-mark in position, make sure it hides the joins in the pages and cover of the book.

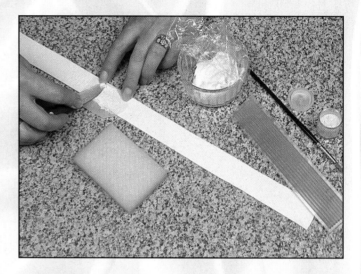

Step 5

Twenty candles were placed on a round board. A musical candle was placed in the centre. A spray of Prunus Blossom was placed around the centre candle.

Emily's 21st Birthday Cake

This cake is dedicated to my darling daughter, who will always be my precious friend.

Roses & Drapes Wedding Cake

A 13" (33cm) hexagonal cake tin and an 18" (46cm) cake board were used for this cake. Both the cake and the board were covered simultaneously in white sugarpaste (rolled fondant).

Step 1

Pleated bows were made for each corner of the cake. Cutter J4-8 was used for the tails. The worktop surface was lightly greased with petal base. Two paste cards were cut out. These were cut out diagonally in half, using a ruler as a guide. This is important as you will require a left and a right side that do not have any petal base on the top side.

Step 2

Place the diagonal pieces back to back and trim the pointed corners. Apply lustre dust to the bow pieces at this stage.

Step 3

Fold creases in a fan-like movement into the tails of the bow. Begin at the wide side of the paste. Press the creases together.

Roses & Drapes Wedding Cake
... Continued

Step 4

Strip No.5 is used for the loops of the bow. Cut out a length of paste the same size as the cutter. Trim the edges. Apply lustre dust to the top side of the bow. Turn the bow over and bring the one end into the middle of the paste. Secure with a little gum glue. Bring the remaining side into the middle. Pinch the centres together.

Step 5

The knot in the bow was made using Cutter J5-4. A strip from Strip No.5 could also be used. Cut out a square shape. Lustre the upper side. Crease in a fan-like manner. Lightly pinch both ends together.

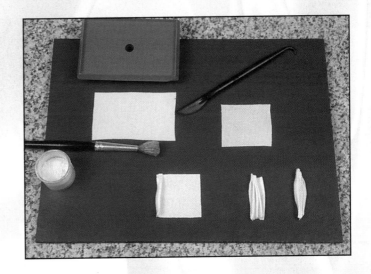

Step 6

Place the knot over the middle of the loops and attach to the back with a little gum glue. Join the loops to the tails.

Roses & Drapes Wedding Cake
... Continued

Step 7

The drapes are made using Strip No.5. Roll out paste on a lightly greased worktop surface. Whilst paste is flat, remember to lustre the top side of the drape. Lightly fold the top strip over exactly in half, making sure you do not crease the paste. Cut out a second strip and repeat.

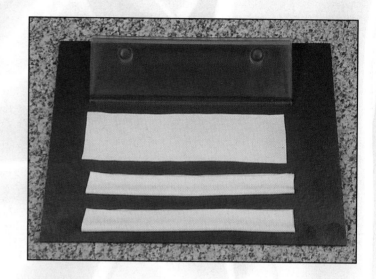

Step 8

The third strip is lustred. Fold over both of the long edges, meeting in the middle of the back of the strip. This will remove the open edges that the previous drape pieces had.

Step 9

Attach the draped strips by applying a little gum glue to the edge of the first layer. Position the second layer. Finally attach the last layer, ensuring that no single, straight edges are visible in the drape. Pinch the ends together.

Roses & Drapes Wedding Cake
... Continued

Step 10

Attach the drapes to the cake from top corner to bottom corner. Use a little gum glue. Attach bows to each corner, neatening the joins.

Step 11

A close-up of the roses on the cake.

Roses & Drapes Wedding Cake

This cake is dedicated to my late niece, Cindy Crutchfield. Cindy was an incredible inspiration to all who knew her as she bravely endured the cancer that robbed her of her young life. We shall always remember you Cindy.

Roses

Roses are possibly the most popular flower used in cake decorating. The size of the cone determines the size of the rose.
For a large life-size rose, a cone approximately this size is needed.

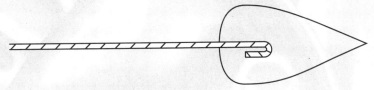

Cones this size require an extra gauge wire to support the flower. The wire should be hooked into the cone. Three or four x 26 gauge wires should be taped together. Cones must be thoroughly dry before any petals are attached.

Every petal should be thinly rolled out. All edges should be 'worked' with a medium ball tool to soften the edges. Do NOT attempt to frill or curl these petals at this stage. You will notice that the extra large petals are rolled out ahead of the other petals. This makes the assembly of the flower easier, as the inside petals are soft and pliable while the outside ones are holding their shape.

Step 1

Place the first petal on the cone by ensuring you have a neat curl around the top of the cone. Do not close the petal against the cone - leave it standing free. The large cutter from Set A10 has been used. Attach the second petal to the cone by joining it to the inside of the first petal. Allow this petal also to stand free of the cone, before easing both the first and then the second petal, closed around the cone.

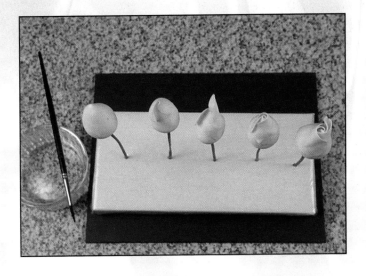

These two steps are important, as they determine how realistic your rose will be. Continue adding more petals to the cone, placing them in the middle of the previous petal in an overlapping position. Keep the petals level with the top of the cone. The number of petals added at this stage could vary between four to seven. The petals are shaded, see Step 2, but are not curled. When attaching the petals to the cone, the side that is shaded is attached to the cone. Water or gum glue may be used to attach the petals.

Roses

... Continued

Step 2

Petal créme is excellent for making roses. It should be used sparingly and applied to wet petals with your fingers. Apply a little yellow to the base of each petal. Work in the colour of your choice to the top half of the petals. Place the petals on a Petal Pad and slightly soften (do not frill) the edges, using Tool 10.

Step 3

Roll out and cut the extra large petals first. You could use twelve or more petals for a large rose. Shade them and curl them with a cocktail stick, away from the colour. Place the petals face down over petal former No.2A. Leave them to partially dry until they are holding their shape.

Step 4

Roll out the middle petals using the cutter in Set B8. Shade and work these petals in the same manner, curling them with a cocktail stick. These petals will be attached to the cone before the extra large petals and should not be as dry. You may use between seven and nine petals this size on a life-size rose.

Roses
... Continued

Step 5
Begin attaching petals to rose made with Set B8. No NOT allow any of these petals to curl backwards at this stage. You may however, allow some 'air space' between the petals.

Step 6
Begin adding the extra large petals that are now partially dry and are holding their shape. Use gum glue to attach the petals. Remember to try to keep petals level with the cone. It may be beneficial to allow the petals to hang upside down as they partially dry.

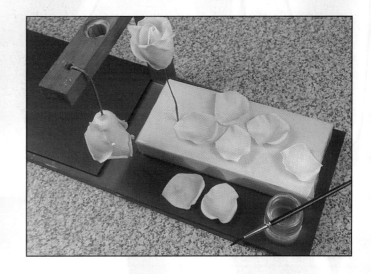

Step 7
When you have sufficient petals attached to the cone, ease petal former 5A over the back of the rose.

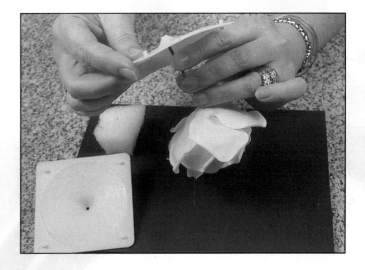

Roses

... Continued

Step 8

The rose resting in the Handy Holder stand. Place sponge foam chips in between the petals and allow the rose to dry.

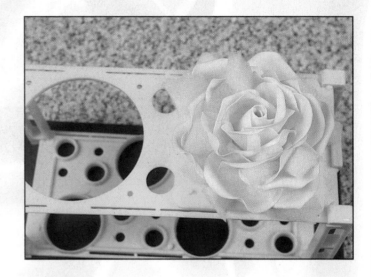

Step 9

Should you wish to highlight the tips of the petals, extra petal créme may be added when the rose is dry. Use a firm paint brush that has a flat base, for this purpose.

Step 10

The Mexican hat principle for a calyx makes a neat hip for the rose. Roll out sufficient green paste to fit over the extra large calyx cutter. This has ready made incisions in it to save the decorator time. Press your fingers against the edge of the cutter, causing the calyx to be cut out. Shade the sepals with a little lustre. (See Step 11). Slightly hollow out the centre.

Roses

... Continued

Step 11

The alternative method of making a calyx. If this method is used, you will need to add a hip by rolling a small ball of green paste and attaching this to the rose after you have secured the calyx to the flower. Shade the sepals with a little lustre.

Step 12

Apply a little gum glue to the middle of the calyx and attach to the rose.

Rose Leaves

Step 13

Roses have a number of different sized leaves on a bush. When rolling out leaves remember to allow for the insertion of taped wire, gauge 26. The new leaves are small and appear in reddish tones, Set L10. The older leaves are fairly large and are dark green, Set B6. When taping the leaves into a sprig, remember the largest leaf is found at the end of the sprig. The leaves are usually found in groups of threes and fives.

Roses

... Continued

Step 14

Life-size roses require an extra large rose leaf from the Large Rose Set. This has been veined with a transparent rose leaf veiner Set V1. This will assist you in placing the veins in the correct position. Place the leaves on a Petal Pad and, using a ball tool, soften the edges. Dry leaves on bubble foam to give them movement

Step 15

When the leaves are dry, dust them with the appropriate petal dust. The edges may be dusted with red dust. Spray them with a cooking spray. This will give them a natural sheen.

Step 16

Rose thorns may be cut out with a thorn cutter found in the Large Rose Set. Attach to the stem using a little gum glue.

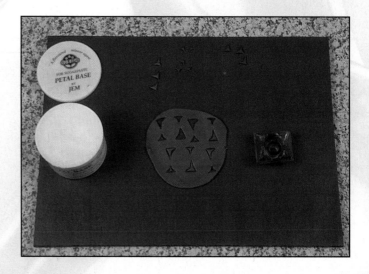

Roses

... Continued

Step 17

A finished rose, illustrating the thorns and leaves.

Step 18

A finished rose that has a petal créme tipped edge.

Step 19

The bud is made using the first row of petals, i.e. the large cutter in Set A10. The middle petals are omitted and the partially dry extra large petals are added ensuring that the base of the cone is completely covered. A calyx is then attached.

Roses

... Continued

Rose Hip

Step 20

A rose hip was made using the large calyx cutter found in Set A10. This was shaded with lustre. A ball of paste was moulded into a hip and placed on the back of the calyx. A cotton centre was shaded with brown petal créme and brown petal dust. This was pulled through the centre to form old stamens. Bend the sepals backwards.

Step 21

The fully developed rose hip. A ball of orange paste slightly larger than a marble has been used. The top of this has been hollowed out using Tool 6. The edges of this indentation were then fingered to create a little edge. Cotton stamens attached to taped wire, gauge 26, were dipped into brown petal créme. They were then pulled through the centre of the hip and fanned out with a sharp instrument. The outside was dusted with brown petal dust. A single sepal was cut out from the extra large calyx cutter and inserted into the middle of the hip.

Step 22

The same principle as above has been used, but this time a full cotton stamen centre is visible with the last remaining petal attached to the calyx. The cotton centre contained four cotton centres taped together. See Steps 23 - 25.

Roses

... Continued

Full Blown Rose

Step 23

To make a cotton centre for a full blown rose, four cotton stamens should be used. Roll cotton around two fingers about 32 times. Grip either side of the cotton with fine wire and secure tightly making sure that the cotton will not pull out. Tape to 26 gauge wire. Bought stamens are available from JEM in different sizes. Trim to required length.

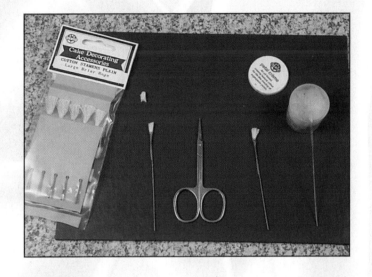

Step 24

Dip the cotton stamens into Sunlover Petal Créme. This will give the stamens body. Use a sharp instrument to separate the stamens. Dip them into brown pollen.

Step 25

Tape four stamen heads together to make the full stamen centre found in an open rose.

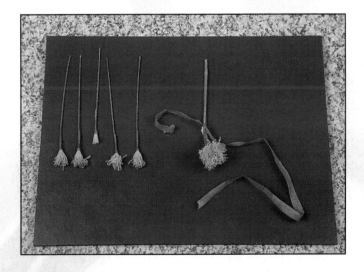

Roses

... Continued

Step 26

Cut out rose petals and work in the same way as mentioned above. Begin assembly with the largest petals that are partially dry. Place a small piece of paste over the centre of petal former 5A. Using gum glue to secure, place the individual petals into position, building up the outside rows and the largest petals first. Use Tool No.6 to secure petals in the centre.

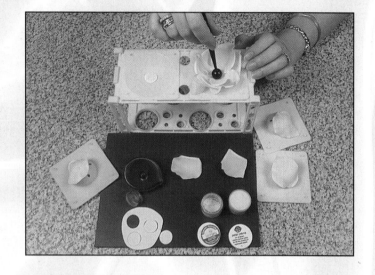

Step 27

Place the middle petals of the rose in position.

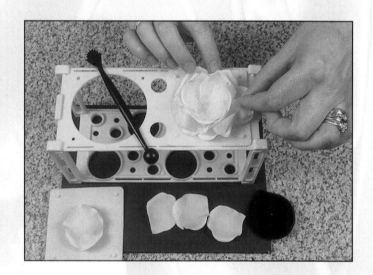

Step 28

Finally place the small petals in position. Apply a little gum glue to the base of the cotton centres and ease the stamens into the middle of the rose. Leave to dry before adding a calyx in the manner described before.

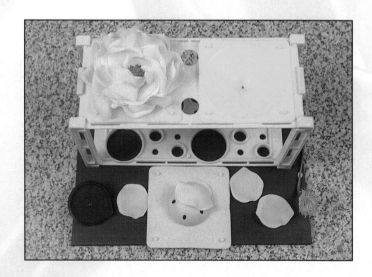

Roses

... Continued

Step 29

A close-up of a full blown rose.

HINT: Cover oasis for dry flower arrangements with plastic cling wrap to avoid particles of oasis making contact with your hands or the flower paste. Insert flower stems into oasis whilst they are drying.

Roses

These roses earned Jill Maytham a bronze in the Master Class - Example of a Plant. Exhibited at the British Sugarcraft 3rd National Exhibition in 1993.

This is dedicated to my precious daughter, Emily Jane.

Neil and Jill's Silver Wedding Anniversary

An 11" (28cm) six petal cake tin was used for this cake. It was placed on a 15" (38cm) round cake board. Both the cake and the board were covered in a pale grey sugarpaste (plastic icing). To balance the large flowers used in this cake, an extra large petal board was made to order. This measured 18" (45cm). This was covered in yellow sugarpaste to match the open roses. This was placed on another 19" (48cm) round cake board which was covered in pale grey. A commercial 25 was used on the cake.

Step 1

The side of the cake boards were covered with double sided tape. Remove the backing of the double sided tape. This will give you an accurate measurement for the amount of ribbon you will require to cover the edge of the cake board.

The thin yellow strip that is in the middle of the wide ribbon was placed against the edge of another strip of double sided tape that still had the backing on it. Cut the excess of this double sided tape away. The wide dark green ribbon used for the edges of the boards was placed on the table. The ends of this ribbon were secured to the table with a little prestik to hold it flat. The backing was removed from the ribbon and the sticky ribbon was placed in position in the middle of the darker ribbon. The combined ribbons were then placed in position on the cake boards.

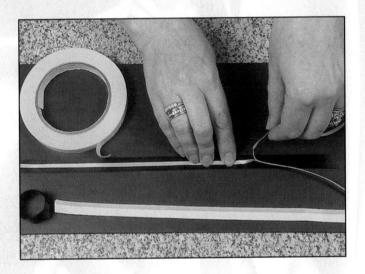

Step 2

The pattern on the end of each petal section of the cake was done with a stencil, JC 5A. Parts of the stencil that were not required were covered with sticky labels. The pattern was then stencilled into position directly on to the cake. White royal icing and a spatula were used for this purpose.

HINT: When taping wire, allow about an extra 1 cm of florist tape to double back on the wire. This will prevent the tape from becoming unravelled.

Neil and Jill's Silver Wedding Anniversary

... Continued

Step 3

Yellow paste was rolled out on to a lightly greased worktop surface. The frill around the base of the cake was made using the large doily cutter and the large disc cutter.

Step 4

A pair of flat bottomed tweezers was used to pinch a crease into the scallop joins to create a simple effect. The frill was attached to the board with a dampened paint brush.

Step 5

A shell was piped in royal icing to neaten the frill joining the cake. The message was cut out using the JEM Alphabet cutters and placed in position on the large petal board before it was secured to the board with a damp paint brush.

Step 6
A close-up of the bougainvillea and open rose.

PETAL BASE
A specially formulated release agent, with a fragrance, for cake decorating.

Neil and Jill's Silver Wedding Anniversary

This cake is a testimony to the living God, to whom we owe everything.

Peace on Earth

A 10" (25cm) oval cake tin was used for this cake. The cake was placed on a 14" (35cm) oval cake board. The cake and the board were covered simultaneously in cream sugarpaste (rolled fondant). An additional cake board was used to display the cake. This measured 16" (40cm). The inside edge of this board was covered in dark green sugarpaste to match the bow and the holly in the cake.

Poinsettia

Step 1

Lightly grease your worktop surface with a little Petal Base. Roll out red paste remembering to allow for the insertion of 26 gauge covered wire. Several petals in each of the different sizes found in Set L5 were used. Vein the petal with rose leaf veiners Set V1. Place the petals on a Petal Pad and using Tool 10 soften the edges of each petal. Allow the petal to set on bubble sponge foam to give them movement.

Step 2

In the same manner, cut out and vein several of the larger cutters in a green paste. Allow for the insertion of 26 gauge taped wire. Place the leaves on Petal Pad and, using Tool 10, lightly soften the edges. Vein with rose leaf veiner Set V1.

HINT: If your hands perspire, dust then with baby powder. This will help keep them cool and dry. Working on a Jem Petal Pad will help alleviate this problem.

Peace on Earth

... Continued

Step 3

Make the stamens for the flower by rolling out a small ball of green paste, smaller than a pea. Form this into a teardrop shape and place it on a 26 gauge wire. Using a small pair of scissors make several incisions into the top of the paste bulb. Paint the ends with red colouring.

Step 4

Twist a few strands of yellow cotton around your finger to form small yellow stamens. Grip the cotton firmly with very fine wire. Pull the yellow stamens into the teardrop you have just made. Tape with shredded $^1/_4$ tape. These stamens slightly protrude.

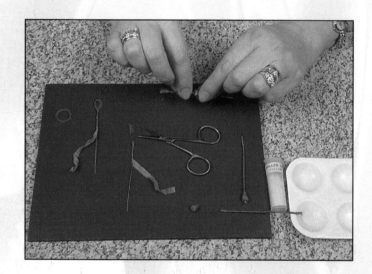

Step 5

Tape flower together using $^1/_2$ width florist tape. Begin with the centre stamens and try not to make the flower symmetrical. Add a few green leaves to one side of the flower.

Peace on Earth

... Continued

Holly Berries

Step 6

Cut out two sizes of holly leaves found in the Set A14. Remember to allow for the insertion of taped wire 26 gauge. Use dark green paste. Vein on holly leaf veiners Set V6.

Step 7

Roll tiny red berries half the size of a pea. Insert a flat hooked wire into the berries. Leave to dry. Spray with a cooking spray to give leaves and berries a sheen. When dry, tape the leaves together forming a holly sprig.

Step 8

Cut out the loops and the tails for the green bow using the same colour dark green paste you will need to make the holly. Strip No.4 was used for this purpose. Curl the loops and the tails around a cylinder shape and allow to set. The inside of a toilet roll is illustrated. When assembling the bow, use gum blue.

Cut out the message and keep it covered until you have cut out a band to fit around the base of the cake. Attach the lettering to the band whilst both the band and the lettering are still soft. Attach the band to the cake with a little water.

Peace on Earth

... Continued

Step 9

The bow on the side of the cake.

Step 10

Cut out the scroll in light beige paste. Curl both ends as desired using a cocktail stick. Using a No.1 nozzle and royal icing, pipe an appropriate message. Leave to dry.

Step 11

A close-up of the poinsettia. The flower on the board helps to balance the arrangement.

Peace on Earth

Peace on Earth

This cake is dedicated to Peter and Jill Frow, in appreciation of their friendship when it was needed most.

Mom's 80th Birthday Cake

This cake was baked in a 16" (40cm) scalloped oval tin. The board was made to fit the tin and measured 20" (50cm). The cake was coated in the usual way with cream coloured sugarpaste (rolled fondant). To mix cream, a little egg yellow and a touch of malt brown was added to a small ball of sugarpaste which was then worked into sufficient sugarpaste to cover the cake and the board.

Step 1

A ribbon was placed on the side of the cake board to reintroduce the colour used in the roses. Double sided tape was placed around the edge of the board. Measure ribbon to the length required. Remove the top layer from the tape and attach the ribbon. Remember to begin at the back of the cake to hide the join. If you are using a paper ribbon, and it is wider than the cake board, insert a pin, level with the cake board into the ribbon and simply tear off the surplus ribbon off. This will leave the ribbon level with the cake board.

Step 2

When the cake is completely dry, position a stencil where the frieze will not hide the stencil pattern. Lightly apply royal icing to the stencil, using a spatula. Be sure to fill all the cavities in the stencil. It is most important that the stencil does not move whilst you apply the royal icing over the pattern. You may find a third hand makes all the difference to achieve success. Use a clean piece of foam sponge and wipe the surplus icing off the stencil. This will assist you in creating a neat even finish.

HINT: Place the lettering on the top of the cake tin. This will help you assess how long your message is and where best to place it in relation to the decoration on the cake.

Mom's 80th Birthday Cake

... Continued

Step 3

Pipe a small reverse shell using a small star tube, a No.6 tube, to seal the cake to the board.

Step 4

Measure the length of the oval frieze you wish to place around the cake and cut out. Trim the edges neatly. The oval frieze used in the cake was dried on the sides of the cake tin that had been lightly greased with Petal Base. Leave to dry completely.

Step 5

Roll out a length of paste and using a ruler or a piece of ribbon as a guide, cut out the length of ribbon required with a pastry wheel. A Pattern was stencilled onto the soft paste ribbon. The ends of the ribbons were trimmed neatly. The ribbon could be lightly dusted with lustre.

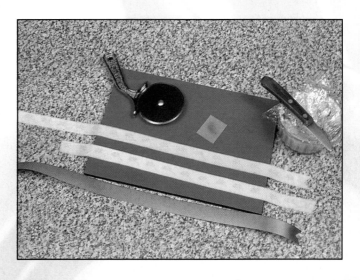

Mom's 80th Birthday Cake

... Continued

Step 6

Thread the ribbon through the frieze whilst it is still soft. Position the dry frieze and ribbon on the cake board. Secure by piping a small shell border using a No.6 tube. Adjust soft ribbon on the board and trim if necessary.

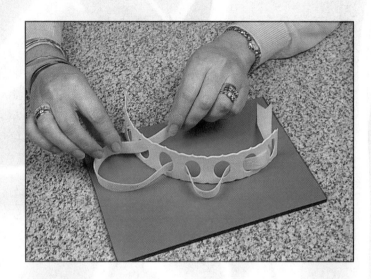

The Fan

To make the fan you may use pastillage which will enable you to display the fan in an upright position, or you may use flower paste. Pastillage is firm, but brittle. Paste is easier to work with, but it is not recommended if you wish to stand the fan in an upright position, as any humidity could cause the fan to collapse.

Sixteen blades have been used to make the fan. It is recommended that you make several more than the required number to allow for breakages. Alternate blades of the fan have been embossed with the JEM Embosser No.1. The remaining blades have been stencilled with royal icing to create an interesting pattern.

*As each pair of blades is cut out, try to avoid moving them as this could distort them. **It is important to remember to cut out a tiny circle through which you can insert the soft taped wire which you will need to hold the fan together whilst assembling it. For this purpose a No.2 icing tube was used to cut the circle.** Remove the little circle whilst the paste is soft. When the blades are dry, if there are any furry edges, remove these with a small piece of fine sandpaper or an emery board.*

Step 7

When assembling the fan, it is recommended that you thread the wire through the hole made in the base of the blade and the ribbon through the body of the blades at the same time. The blades are brittle and it is almost impossible to go back to thread the ribbon through at a later stage. Only the double insertions in the blades have ribbon threaded through them. The other cut is merely to add to the decoration.

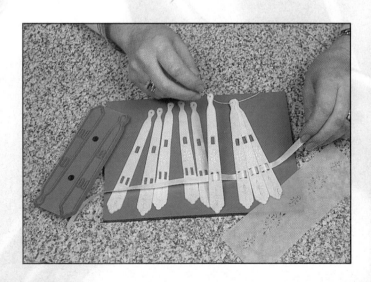

Mom's 80th Birthday Cake

... Continued

Step 8
To hide the wire loop on the fan, make a bow the same width as the paste ribbon threaded through the oval frieze. Cut sufficient paste for one loop of the bow and then the other. Place both the loops together and then position another piece of ribbon over the loops to form the knot.

Step 9
The finished fan showing Embosser No.1.

Note:
The lettering was cut out using the JEM alphabet set. When cutting out lettering, the paste should be thin, but not too thin. Roll out your flower paste on a worktop surface lightly greased with Petal Base. The lettering could be shaded whilst still soft, and before it is picked up off the worktop surface. Carefully place in position on the cake using a little water to attach to the cake.

Mom's 80th Birthday Cake

Mom's 80th Birthday Cake

This cake is dedicated to my mother, Joan McLachlan, who has been my best friend all my life.

Engagement Forever Yours

Two 11" (28cm) heart shaped cake tins were used for this cake. The cakes were covered separately on spare boards and allowed to dry. A modest bust was moulded onto the female cake and this was covered in flesh coloured sugarpaste (rolled fondant). The male was covered in white. A board was specially made and coated in cream sugarpaste.

Step 1

A heart shaped pattern was made about 1cm larger than the tin. A mixture of two thirds sugarpaste and one third flower paste was made and coloured for the bodice. A piece of guipure lace was placed over the bodice. A plastic traycloth is an alternative suggestion. A large plastic tube roller was used to gently emboss the pattern onto the bodice. Apply even pressure. Cut out heart using pattern after embossing sugarpaste.

Step 2

A large fancy oval plaque cutter P2 was used to cut out the neckline. Darts were made using Tool 4B. Lift up the bodice and place in position on the cake.

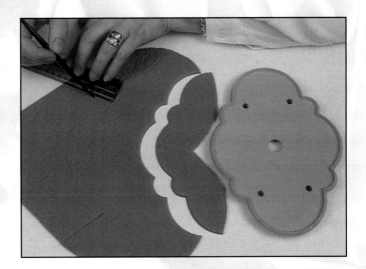

HINT: A variety of worktop surfaces are suitable - panelite board, glass or a ceramic tile are a few suggestions.

Engagement Forever Yours

... Continued

Step 3

Roll out flower paste on lightly greased worktop surface. A gold chain to decorate the female was made using Strip 1. This was dusted gold and then twisted around a narrow perspex rod. Place in position whilst damp and attach to the cake with a little gum glue.

Step 4

Measure the required length of the man's shirt. Cut out the double sided frill cutter F5, to make the ruffle on the man's shirt. Lightly press Strip 1 into the frill to create the impression of tucks. Flute the edges of both sides to cause it to appear ruffled, using Tool 15A.

Step 5

Cut strips using frill cutter F1A to widen the ruffle or you may cut the double sided frill in half. Frill the strips, causing the edges to appear ruffled using Tool 15A. Trim the base of the ruffle.

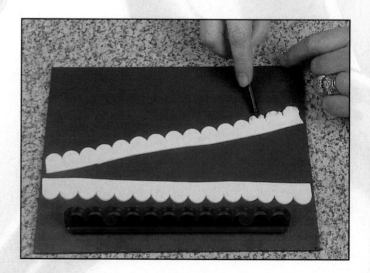

Step 6

Make the bow tie using black flower paste. Fold over two equal pieces of sponge foam to form the loops of the bow. Cut another band to form the knot. Assemble the bow using gum glue, whilst still soft and allow to dry.

Step 7

Place the bow in position at the top of the ruffle. Cut out black and white buttons using the daisy centre stamps. Secure with a little gum glue. Tip white edges of buttons using gold dust mixed with a drop of alcohol.

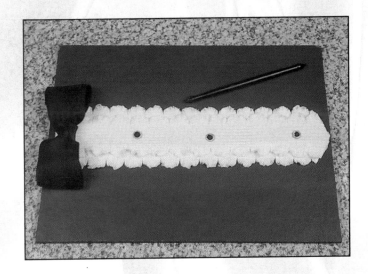

Step 8

Cut out a paper pattern for the man's jacket. Mix black flower paste and cut out the jacket. Turn the pattern over for the other side. Use a pastry wheel to cut out, as a knife will cause the paste to distort. Place in position on the man's cake. A dressmaker's wheel was used to create the stitches.

Engagement Forever Yours
... Continued

Step 9

Cut out a card using card cutter J4-7. Cut out the He and She cutters from Set J6-12 in black to create a silhouette effect.

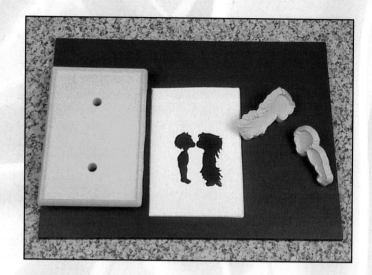

Step 10

In a contrasting colour, cut out a picture frame using Set J4-2. J5-4 will cut out the middle forming the edge of the frame.

Step 11

The decorations around the edge of the hearts were made from the double heart side cutter. These were place over an object that has a right angle and left to dry. An ice cream box was used.

Engagement Forever Yours
... Continued

Step 12
A close-up of the side of the cake.

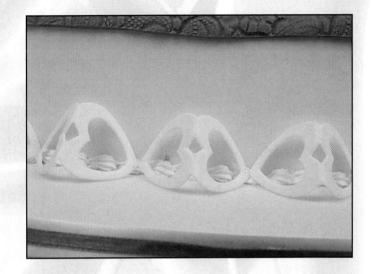

Carnation
Step 13
Lightly grease worktop surface with Petal Base. Cut out two layers for each carnation using the Carnation/Round Plaque Cutter. Tool 13A is used to make slits into the scallops on the edge of the cutter. Tool 12 is used to frill the edges.

Step 14
Frill two layers for each carnation. Place the one on top of the other. Fold the double layer in half. Place a little gum glue in the centre of the folded portion below the frilled edge. Pick up the flower in your hands and push the sides together creating a gathered effect with frilled edges.

Engagement Forever Yours
... Continued

Step 15
Trim the surplus form the flower. Insert a hooked 20 gauge taped wire into the base of the flower.

Step 16
To colour the tips of the carnation, the edges are dipped into a mixture of pure alcohol that has had some food colouring added to it. This will colour the paste effectively and it will dry quickly as the alcohol evaporates. Avoid working with alcohol in a confined area as the fumes are unpleasant. Shake off surplus alcohol.

Step 17
The calyx for the carnation is made from the hibiscus calyx found in Set B14. A second calyx is attached to the base of the flower. This is taken from the sweetpea Set B17.

Engagement Forever Yours

... Continued

Step 18

The sword fern to go with the carnation is found in Set L2B. This leaf is rolled out on a lightly greased worktop surface and cut out flat.

Step 19

Place the leaf on a Petal Pad and, using a tool of your choice (Tool 4A is illustrated), work each section of the leaf, causing it to curl slightly. Alternatively, the individual leaves may be worked from the outside towards the centre, using a small ball tool. Use Tool 4B to vein each leaf.

Step 20

A 26 gauge wire covered in green tape is lightly covered with gum glue. Remove excess glue. Place wire at the top of the leaf and, using fingers, press into position down the centre of the leaf and leave to dry.

Engagement Forever Yours

... Continued

Step 21

Tape cutter with two blades removed showing tape cut in half. Use this to bind sword fern and carnation into corsage.

Step 22

Singapore orchid corsage. Instructions for Singapore orchid may be found on page 146.

HINT: Store flower paste in the fridge if not in use.

Before beginning to make a flower, "work" the paste thoroughly to ensure that it is pliable.

Paste should stretch and not crumble.

If paste is too dry, add a little egg white to it.

If paste is too sticky, a little white vegetable fat rubbed on your hands should help.

Engagement Forever Yours

On your Engagement

145

Singapore Orchid (denrobium)

Step 1

Roll paste into a tiny ball, less than the size of a pea. Shape this into a cone. Using Tool No.4A, slightly hollow out the cone to form the column of the orchid. A taped 25 gauge wire should be inserted into the top lower half of the column at a 45° angle, leaning towards the back pointed part of the column. Lightly grease worktop surface using Petal Base and cut out the front of the orchid, (the labellum), using the Singapore Cutters.

Step 2

This is not a frilly orchid. Use Tool 4A to make a few small frills at the top edge of the labellum. The lobes of the labellum may be cupped slightly with a small ball tool. Vein the throat of the trumpet lightly, using the veining tool 4B. Place the column into the middle of the petal, using a little gum glue to secure. Leave to dry.

Step 3

Roll out the lateral sepals. Vein each sepal with a corn leaf veiner, Set V5.

Singapore Orchid
... Continued

Step 4

Place the sepals on a petal pad and, using
Tool 10, slightly soften the edges. Using the
tool, stretch the base of the sepals slightly.

Step 5

Cut out the side petals. Vein and soften the
edges as described above. Using a little gum
glue, attach petals to sepals as illustrated.
Insert dry centre into the middle of the sepals,
ensuring that the base of the column will fit
into the corner of the sepals. Lift up both
sides of the lateral sepals so that they firmly
grip the base of the trumpet.

Step 6

Place the flower over a petal former, A1, as
illustrated. Petal former A2 would also be
suitable and would create a flower opening
at a different stage. Note the bud drying in
a hanging down position on the Handy
Holder. This is made by attaching a centre
to the sepals. The sepals are then
encouraged to close, forming a bud. The
back of the dry orchid is tipped light green.
The throat base is carefully tipped with a little
orange dust. The remaining throat is lightly
shaded with a little pale yellow petal dust.
A little lustre may be used on the orchid.

Singapore Orchid
... Continued

Step 7

The small orchid cutters are illustrated, as well as the closed bud, described in Step 6.

Step 8

A mixed spray of large and small Singapore orchids. (Acknowledgement to Pam Milne).

Singapore Orchid

A spray of Singapore orchids on a sugarpaste (rolled fondant) log. This display is dedicated to my precious son, Michael Neil.

Michael's 21st Birthday Cake

A key shaped tin was used for this cake. The board was made to order. The cake and the board were covered separately in cream sugarpaste (rolled fondant). The cake was left to dry on a spare board, covered with wax paper, for several days before the key was placed in position. The cake was secured to the board with a little royal icing. Strip No.5 was used for the wide band around the cake. This was trimmed with Strip No.3. Notes for the acorns shown in this cake may be found on page 86.

A 6" (15cm) round board was covered in red paste. A doily cutter and a disc cutter were used to create a band of red and white. A musical candle was secured to the middle of the board with a royal icing star. Twenty stars were evenly spaced around the board piped in royal icing to support the remaining twenty candles.

Step 1

Measure the circumference of the beer can and cut out sufficient paste to wrap around the can. Keep the paste covered with cling wrap to prevent it from drying out, until you have made all the cutouts for the label. The label on the beer can was made using Cutter No. J4-7 as an impression only. The outline of the label was cut out using a light beige paste and Strip No.2.

Step 2

The red band was made using strip No.5. This was trimmed to size using the edge of the same cutter. The word 'Castle' was cut out in white paste using the JEM Alphabet cutters. The message on the cake was cut out in red paste to add colour to the cake.

Michael's 21st Birthday Cake
... Continued

Step 3

The detail on the can was made using strips of paste in beige and red paste. Strip No.1 was used. A sharp scalpel was used to make close incisions in this strip. These strips were cut to the appropriate lengths. Stretch the strips slightly and attach to the label to create the impression of lettering.

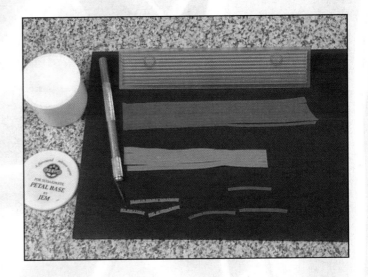

Step 4

The castle on the band was made using red paste and the small square cutter from the geometrical quilting patch designs. Strips No. 2 and 3 were used to make the towers.

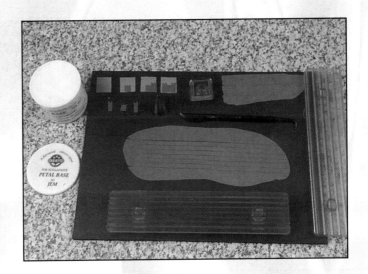

Step 5

Measure the circumference of a beer can. Cover the beer can with wax paper. Using a little gum glue, attach the lettering and other trimmings to the can. Place the label around the can allowing the joins to meet at the back of the can. Do not attempt to stick the joins together. Leave to set. Make a lid for the can and colour it with a little silver dust mixed with a drop of alcohol or a little cocoa butter.

Michael's 21st Birthday Cake

... Continued

Step 6

A pattern shorter than an actual tie was made. Cut out paste for the tie and the appropriate decorations. Strips No.1 and 2 are illustrated, as is the '0' from the numeral set A1 and the miniature reindeer from the Christmas Miniature Set No.1. Attach the decoration whilst it is still damp, using a damp paint brush. Drape the tie over the cake and leave to dry.

Step 7

Position the beer can and secure to cake board with a little royal icing. The beer froth was made from a recipe for sugar rocks. This was carefully poured into the moulded top of the can and allowed to spill over. See Sugar Rocks recipe.

HINT: A table lamp will help to hasten the drying time your work needs.

Michael's 21st Birthday Cake

This cake dedicated to my beloved son, Michael, who will always have a special place in my heart.

Angela ... With Love

An 11" (28cm) round cake tin was used for this cake. The cake was coated in the normal way in white sugarpaste (rolled fondant). A stencilled pattern was used on the side of the cake. (See instructions on page 123.)

Step 1

The frill at the base of the cake was made from the large JEM Doily Cutter (160mm) and the large round disk cutter (120mm). Lightly grease your worktop surface with Petal Base and roll out your paste not too thinly. Choose a contrasting colour for the best effect. Cut out the doily. Place the disc cutter in the centre and cut out a circle. The remaining edge will create a frill.

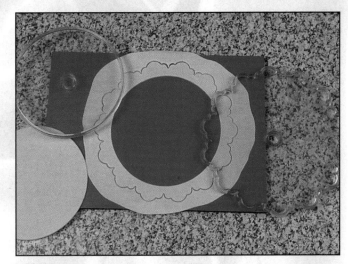

Step 2

Using a pair of tweezers pinch a crease into the frill at the lowest points. To add interest, use Embosser No.1 to press a pattern into the frill. Measure the circumference of the cake and cut out the required number of frills to place around the side of the cake and on the cake board. Use a little water to attach the frill to the cake and to the board.

Step 3

The frill in position. A small royal icing snail's trail piped with a No.2 nozzle or a small star tube, neatens the join at the base of the cake. A stencil was used on the side of the cake.

Angela ... With Love

... Continued

Step 4

Jasmine, carnations and a rose spray. See instructions elsewhere for these flowers.

HINT: When arranging flowers on a cake, NEVER push wires into the icing. This is most unhygienic and should be remembered at all times!

Angela ... With Love

This cake is dedicated to my sister-in-law, Angela McLachlan.

Porcelain Roses

A 14$\frac{1}{2}$" (37cm) flat top diamond cake tin was used for this cake. The cake was cut in half using the corner of the tin as a guide. This created a two tier effect. The square cake was placed on a cake board made slightly larger than the cake. This was covered at the same time as the cake.

A candlestick holder was used to support the cake. The narrow cake was covered separately in cream sugarpaste (rolled fondant) and left to dry on a spare cake board. A cake board was made to order creating a 3" (7cm) border around the cake tin. The large board was covered in cream sugarpaste and allowed to dry.

Step 1

Cream paste was rolled out on lightly greased worktop surface. The Double Square side cutter was used to cut out sufficient pieces to form the design on the side of the cake. Allow the paste to air dry for a short period before lifting out the centre square pieces. This will prevent distortion of the square shape. Place the double squares over a right angle to dry. A polystyrene ice cream box is illustrated.

Step 2

Lightly grease worktop surface with a little Petal Base. Cut out a bow Size No.2 for each corner of the cake.

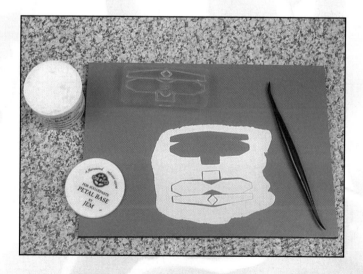

HINT: Store finished work in a sealed container. Ensure that both are thoroughly dry before storing.

Porcelain Roses

... Continued

Step 3

Fold the loops into the centre and secure with a little water or gum glue. Neaten the join with the little knot. Place the loops on top of the tails and allow to dry. The dry bows were shaded with aquamarine petal dust.

Step 4

The rose leaves Set B6 were cut out in cream paste. Provision was made for the insertion of gauge 26 wire taped in white florist tape. The leaves were veined with Rose leaf veiners Set V1 and allowed to dry.

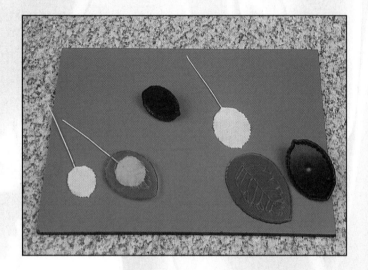

Step 5

The dry leaves were dusted with aquamarine petal dust. They wre sprayed with a cooking spray and allowed to dry. The leaf edges were tipped gold. The gold dust was mixed with a drop of alcohol.

Porcelain Roses

... Continued

Step 6

A close-up of the side of the cake.

Instructions for making the roses appear on page 111.

HINT: If you live in humid conditions, a cupboard with an electric light bulb fitted in the base is an excellent way to store and preserve flowers or foliage. The cupboard should have small vent holes at the top to allow the hot air to escape.

Porcelain Roses

This cake is dedicated to Jane McLachlan, Megan's precious mother.

Bougainvillea Wedding Cake

A 12" (30cm) square cake tin was used for this cake. The cake board measured 15" (38cm). A pattern was made approximately 5" (13cm) deep to remove a corner of the cake thereby creating the effect of a two tier cake. Cream sugarpaste was used to coat the cake. Use a little egg yellow to colour sugarpaste cream. The bottom tier and the cake board were covered simultaneously. The cut out section of the cake was covered on a spare cake board which was covered with grease-proof paper and left to dry for two days. It was then placed in position, lining up with the back corner of the cake.

A royal icing shell was piped around the base of the cake and the top tier, using a No.7 star nozzle.

Step 1

The JEM Frieze No.1 was used to make the windows. Lightly grease your worktop surface with Petal Base. Measure the side of the cake and evenly roll out sufficient paste to cut out the windows. Two panels of five and nine windows respectively were cut out and allowed to dry flat. To avoid distorting the windows allow them to 'skin' dry before removing the inner pieces. Two further panels containing six windows each were cut out and dried on a round 9" (23cm) cake tin that had been lightly greased with Petal Base.

To position the dry panels on the cake and the cake board, a small shell, using a No.5 nozzle, was piped onto the cake board. The panels were then gently pushed up against the shell and allowed to dry.

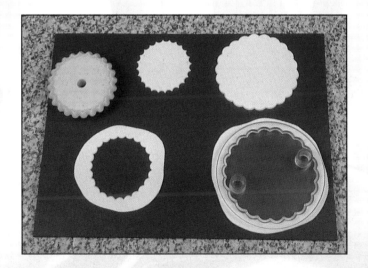

Step 2

The platform for the bride and groom was constructed by cutting out two scalloped discs. The base scallop was J4-5 and the top was the Carnation Plaque Cutter. These were cut out and allowed to dry.

Bougainvillea Wedding Cake

... Continued

Step 3

Strip 5 was used to cut out the wide band for the sides of the platform. This was dried around a plastic lid taken from a spray can. The lid was lightly greased with Petal Base. The base scallop was barely visible, creating an extended platform edge for the display of the bride and groom.

The platform was assembled with royal icing and left to dry.

Step 4

The bride and groom on the raised platform. To dress the bride and groom, see instructions on page 167.

Bougainvillea

Step 5

You will need to make centre in several sizes for the different bougainvillea bracts. Three 26 gauge wires are needed for each cluster of bracts. These should be covered in a quarter width green florist tape. Roll out a tiny ball of paste, the same colour as the bracts. Place the paste at the top of the wire and roll the paste between your fingers, forming a shaped column that has a bulbous base. The smaller bracts do not have flowers on their tops.

Bougainvillea Wedding Cake

... Continued

Step 6

The fully developed bracts are made in the same way as described before. However, to incorporate the little flowers that appear on some of the these centres, it is necessary to include taping a stamen that has a little yellow blossom attached to it before forming the centre. Use the smallest baby daisy cutter No.0 for these flowers. Roll out the paste in the usual way. Place flowers on a Petal Pad. Use Tool No.10 or similar to lightly frill and cup the flower. Insert a stamen, that has been dipped into a little gum glue, into the centre of the flower. Tape to wire and shape column.

Step 7

The bracts illustrated in the picture were made with set B23. Smaller bracts were also included in the spray and were made with a miniature orchid lateral sepal cutter and a snowdrop cutter from set B16. The Mexican hat principle was used to add strength to the base of the bracts. Place the 'hat' over the centre of the cutter and, using your fingers, apply pressure to the edge of the cutter causing the bracts to be cut out. Tool 10 was used to soften the edges on a Petal Pad. The smaller bracts do not require visible centres and will therefore only require a single wire.

Step 8

Place the centre into the middle of the bracts. Lift each bract up, ensuring that the centre is still visible.

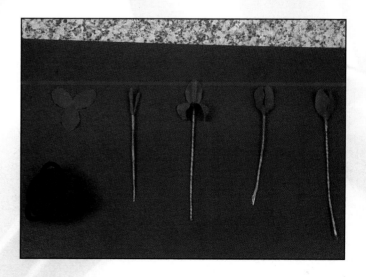

Bougainvillea Wedding Cake

... Continued

Step 9

The smaller bougainvillea cutter found in Set L6A is illustrated. Cut out the bracts in the usual way. Vein each bract using a rose leaf veiner Set V1. Lightly fold the base of each bract backwards and allow it to dry on an upside down petal former No.3B. Cut out the required number of bracts and shape in the same way.

Step 10

When all the bracts are dry, beginning with the centre, position the bracts evenly, firmly gripping each bract with florist tape.

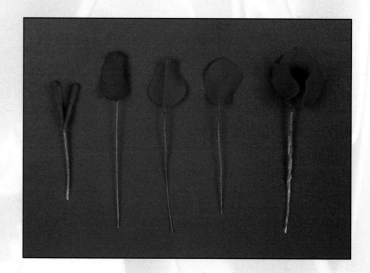

Step 11

The largest bract is veined and worked in the same way as described in Step 9 and Step 10. When taping the little yellow flowers into the centres, remember to vary the number of flowers in each cluster of bracts for a more realistic effect.

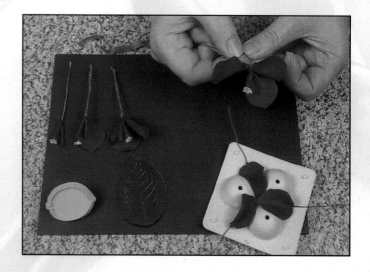

Bougainvillea Wedding Cake
... Continued

Step 12

Leaves we made using a dark green paste. These leaves were taken from Set B33. The leaves were veined with the rose veiner Set V1. They were dusted with dark green dust and sprayed with a cooking spray to give them a sheen. Allow to dry.

Step 13

Tape the various sizes of bougainvillea clusters together into a number of sprays incorporating the leaves.

Bougainvillea Wedding Cake

This cake is dedicated to my dear friend and assistant, Elsie Stapylton-Adkins. Elsie and I spent many happy hours together, encouraging one another as we worked together creating the flowers and decorations found in this book.

Bride and Groom

The Tylose Recipe for flower paste was used with an equal portion of sugarpaste (rolled fondant) to make the bride and groom. The paste was shaded with a little coppertone food colouring to create flesh.

Step 1

Using Petal Base, lightly grease the moulds. Take a ball of paste, sufficient to fit into the mould and shape it into an oval. Rub Petal Base very well all over the oval 'body'. To ensure you obtain a good impression of the face, press the point of the oval into the nose of the mould. Press paste evenly and firmly into the one half of the mould before placing the back over the paste. Press mould together firmly and release body.

Carefully hollow out the base of the dress to facilitate the drying process. Rub Petal Base over a cocktail stick and insert a cocktail stick up into the head of the mould to help it stay in position whilst it dries. This will be removed when the figure is dry.

NB: Allow the mould to partially dry before cutting the arms free from the body to enable dressing. Leave the mould to dry for 24 hours before attempting to trim the surplus paste away.

Step 2

To paint the eyes, petal dust was mixed with a little alcohol. To prevent the paint from cracking, dip the paint brush into a little Dishwashing liquid before applying the paint to the eye. Paint the socket white. When the socket is dry, paint the eyeball black. Allow to dry and then paint a white dot in the centre of the eyeball. Apply a little pale blue eye shadow above the eye. Carefully outline the eye in brown using a fine paint brush.

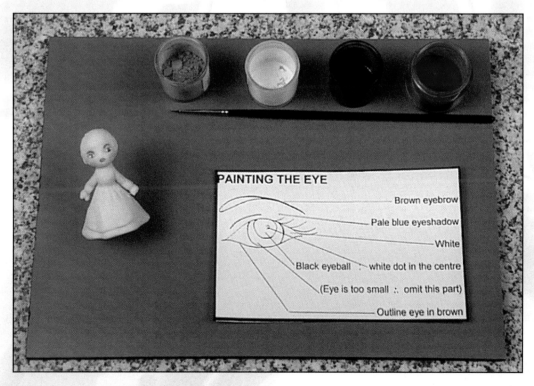

PAINTING THE EYE

— Brown eyebrow
— Pale blue eyeshadow
— White
Black eyeball :. white dot in the centre
(Eye is too small :. omit this part)
— Outline eye in brown

Bride and Groom

... Continued

Step 3

Two different shades of royal icing were used to paint on the hair. Do not mix the colours through. The variation of colour gives the hair highlights.

Step 4

Lightly grease your worktop surface with Petal Base and roll out the wedding dress thinly. Use the Carnation Plaque cutter to cut out the skirt. Use a size 3 daisy stamp or an icing nozzle to cut out the waist. This must be off centre creating a longer back for the dress.

Use lustre dust on the skirt and bodice whilst it is still damp. This will create a satin effect.

Step 5

Using the short friller, Tool 15A, frill the edge of the skirt. Using Tool 13A, cut the skirt down the middle of the back.

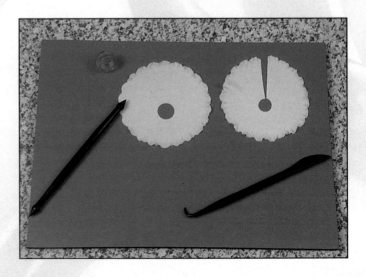

Bride and Groom

Dedicated to Samantha and Garth Anderson, Emily's special friends.

Chocolate Box

A 10" (25cm) square cake was baked for this cake. It was covered with marzipan and sugarpaste (rolled fondant) in the usual way. The cake was placed to the side of a 14" (35cm) board, covered with gold paper. To add interest and balance to the presentation, an 18" gold board was also used.

Step 1

The lid of the box was made from a 10" (25cm) square cake board. The cake board was covered with sugarpaste (rolled fondant) on both sides. This was allowed to dry completely. The sides of the lid were made using JEM Cutter endless frill F1B which has a serrated edge. A number of 50's were cut out. Cream and gold 50's were placed on the lid to create interest to the top of the box.

The joins on top of the lid were hidden using the JEM strip cutter, No.2.

The same endless frill cutter was used to trim the top of the box, i.e. the top of the cake. A stencil was used on the front of the box to take away the bleakness of the box.

Step 2

The dry lid was placed in position at the back of the cake. A length of sugarpaste (rolled fondant) in the same colour as the box was rolled out and secured to the sugarpaste (rolled fondant) at the edge of the back of the cake with a little royal icing. The lid was then supported in position and allowed to dry. Two little plaques were cut out and trimmed to fit into the angle on the side of the lid to support it. Whilst the icing was drying, a little jar was used to hold the lid in position.

HINT: Never roll out too much paste. Roll out only sufficient for the petals you need to cut out.

Chocolate Box

... Continued

Step 3

The chocolate cups were made using flower paste to create an assortment of chocolates to place in the box. Cutter No.J4-6 was used for this purpose. A little cornflour was placed in the chocolate mould and a small bottle was used to press the paste against the impression of the chocolate mould. Other chocolate was melted into chocolate moulds to fill the box. Place the chocolates in the box, reserving a couple to add interest to the open gift wrap.

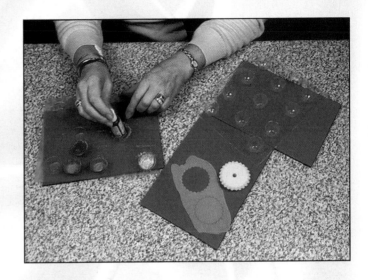

Gift Wrap

Step 4

A paper pattern was made, by actually covering the cake tin with brown paper and wrapping a parcel. The pattern for the folds in the back of the box was cut from this (see step 6). The square base of the cake was removed from the pattern and the remaining pattern was cut out in sugarpaste in three parts creating the two sides of the parcel and the narrow strip in front of the box. The narrow strip was placed upside down on the cake board, as it represents the paper from under the box.

Step 5

The geometrical patterns from JEM were used to make the gift wrap. Colours suitable for a man were chosen, and a selection of patterns was planned for the 'paper'. Numerous pieces were cut out in different colours, and kept damp by covering them with cling wrap until they were needed. The basic colour was rolled out in flower paste, on Petal Base, to ensure that it would not stick to the worktop surface. The patterns were slightly dampened with a little water and placed on the flower paste. Avoid excess water, it will mark your 'paper'. Press patterns down with a flat board.

Chocolate Box
... Continued

Step 6

Cut out 'gift wrap' according to pattern for the back of the cake and, using a little water, attach it to the cake, creating the effect of a wrapped parcel.

Now cut out the top sides of the gift wrap and again attach to the sides of the box with a little water. To hold the paper up to create an open parcel effect, use pieces of foam to support it until it is dry. See finished cake.

Step 7

To make the wide ribbon that falls over the cake, roll out white flower paste to give you sufficient length to hang over the cake. Measure the desired width and, using a pastry wheel, cut the length. A ruler or a board will assist you in cutting out a straight line. An actual ribbon placed over your flower paste could also assist you in cutting out a wide ribbon in a straight line. Keep this covered with cling wrap, until you have rolled out two shades of flower paste to form the stripes in the ribbon. Use the JEM Strip No.2 endless cutter for the stripes. Apply a little water to the back of the cut strips and, using a ruler to assist you in keeping the strips straight, apply a little pressure to secure the strips.

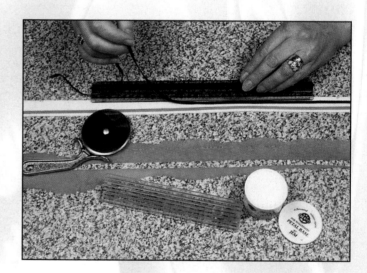

Step 8

Cut short lengths of this ribbon to make the loops for this parcel. Use a little foam to shape the loops until they are dry. Drape the longer ribbon pieces over the cake and leave to dry in position on the cake. When the lops are dry, position on the cake. Secure with a little royal icing.

Chocolate Box

... Continued

Step 9

The message was written over several name cards. (Set J5-2)

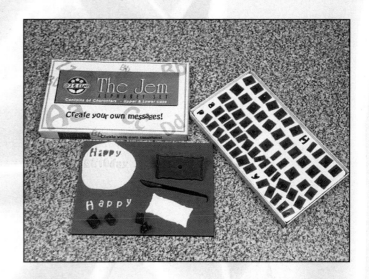

Step 10

To keep the message in a straight line, place a marker on the plaque as a guide. The colours used in the cake were reintroduced in these name cards to balance the use of colour.

HINT: When painting 'dots' onto petals, a cocktail stick is easier to use than a paint brush, as it does not bend.

Chocolate Box

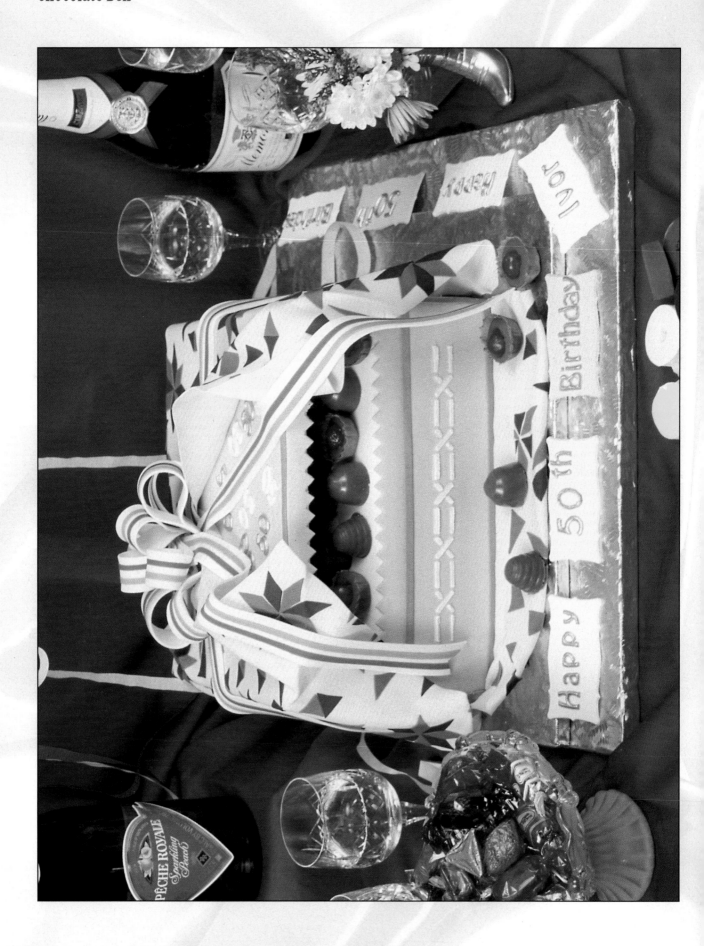

This cake is dedicated to Ivor Migdoll, who did the photography for this book.

A Striking Effect

A set of flat top diamond tins were used for this cake.
Cover the cake in the usual way and leave to dry completely for two or three days.
Cover the sides of the cake board with ribbon of your choice. Using double sided sticky tape will simplify this task.

Note: Colour your paste black by using sufficient black colouring. Paste colouring may be used or if you use powder colouring, mix it with a little alcohol. You may need to add more Tylose to your paste as the amount of colouring used does cause the consistency of the paste to become very soft.

Step 1

Cut out JEM Double Square Side Pattern and allow to dry flat. Make a paper pattern to mark the position of these side pieces on the cake.

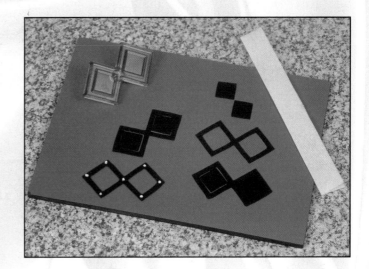

Step 2

Using a little white royal icing, attach to sides of cake, making sure you position the patterns in the correct place. Pipe a shell border in black royal icing, using a No.7 nozzle, around the base of the cake.

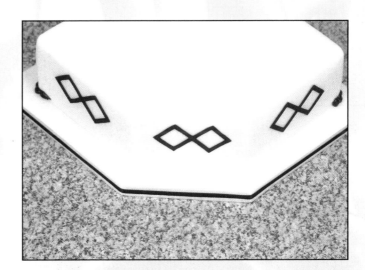

HINT: When using a large cutter, apply even pressure over the total area to ensure achieving a clean egde.

A Striking Effect

... Continued

Step 3

Using a JEM medium bow cutter, cut out sufficient bows. In this case, two bows have been used on either side of the side design. Leave to dry. Attach with a little white royal icing

Step 4

The five petal daisy wheel cuter was used to make the white filler flowers. Tiny buds were shaped onto the end of a stamen.

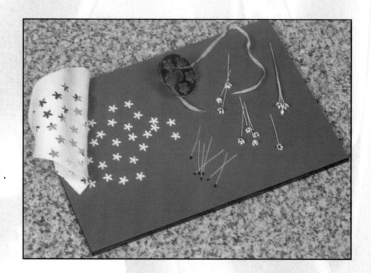

Step 5

The eight petal daisy wheel cutter was used for the black filler flowers. Shredded white florist tape was used to combine the black and white sprays.

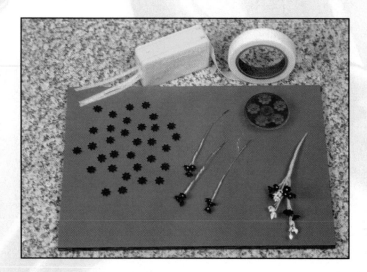

A Striking Effect

... Continued

Cattleya Orchid

Step 6

Using a firm wire gauge 24, cover with white tape and slightly bend the one end. Cover the curved tip with a little paste and then, using Set JEM B30, cut out a column which will neaten the centre of the labellum (throat)

Step 7

Cut out the labellum (throat) using JEM B1. Vein, using a JEM orchid veiner. A "V" may be cut out of the middle of the centre. Frill the edges of the petal, using the veining/frilling tool, JEM Tool No.12. Using a little Tylose glue, attach the column to the labellum (throat).

Step 8

Place the labellum (throat) into JEM flower former 4A and leave to dry. If necessary prop up the sides with small pieces of foam.

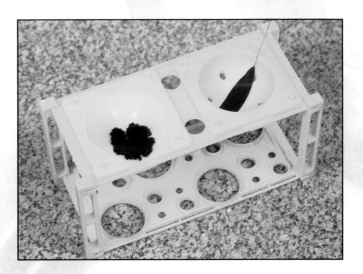

A Striking Effect

... Continued

Step 9

Cut out the side petals. Remember to allow a ridge of paste for the insertion of your wire gauge 26 which should be covered with white tape. Vein with orchid veiner and frill the edges using JEM No.12 Tool or similar. Shape petals over flower former 1A. Leave to dry.

Step 10

Cut out three back sepals allowing for the insertion of the wire gauge 26, covered in white tape. Vein with JEM corn leaf veiner Set V5. Shape petals over JEM flower former and leave to dry.

Step 11

When the orchid petals are dry, tape together. Begin with the two side petals, then the outer petals and finally ease the centre into position. Make sure the petals are firmly taped together. The edges of the petals may be lightly tipped with a gold lustre dust, if desired, at this stage.

A Striking Effect

... Continued

Step 12

The finished spray taped together with the orchid in the centre. Note how the side sprays have been bent. Using a little white royal icing on stem of spray, position and attach to cake surface.

HINT: When frilling or fluting petals, pick up the petal constantly to enable it to stretch. This will create the frilled effect desired.

Best Wishes Pam & Ian

A Comma Cake Tin was used for this cake, 10" (25cm) long and 7" (18cm) wide. The cake was placed on a 14" (35cm) oval cake board. The cake and board were coated in the usual way in white sugarpaste (rolled fondant).

Lace Pieces

Step 1

Lace pieces to go around the top edge of the cake were cut out using the King's Lace Cutter. Grease your worktop surface fairly well with Petal Base. Position the paste and then roll out sufficient paste to cut out about 5 strips of lace. Paste should be even and not too thin. Cut out the lace pieces. To prevent the lace pieces from distorting, allow the paste surrounding the cut lace pieces to skin dry before removing surplus paste. Remove the centre of the lace with a sharp instrument.

Step 2

Filler flowers using a multiple daisy cutter were used for the orchid spray. The flowers were placed on a piece of sponge foam and an impression was made on them using the Daisy Point Tool No.16B. Cotton stamens were dipped into gum glue and inserted through the centre of the flowers. They were allowed to dry before being taped into a spray. Tiny buds were shaped onto the ends of the cotton stamens.

Step 3

A close-up of the orchid and filler flower. Orchid instructions may be found on page 146.

Best Wishes Pam & Ian

Best Wishes Pam & Ian

This cake is dedicated to my favourite Uncle and Aunt, Ian and Pam Whytock. Their love and support have always been appreciated.

Frangipani Wedding Cake

An oval tin 15 1/2" (39cm) was used for this cake. A pattern was made creating two commas out of the oval tin. These formed the top two tiers. The base of this cake is a dummy made to order. The cakes were cut out carefully and coated in marzipan. To strengthen the narrow tips in this cake the marzipan was left to dry on a spare cake board for 48 hours. The cakes were then coated individually in sugarpaste (rolled fondant) and left to dry for a further 48 hours before being placed on cake boards that were made to order. Cover the cake boards separately and allow to dry.

Commercial white plastic pillars were used to support this cake. Before they were placed in position a clean thin dowel stick was inserted into each pillar. This was then eased into the cake until it touched the cake board. If it is necessary, trim to make it level with the top of the pillar.

Step 1

The paper patterns were designed to fit into the oval tin. This idea could be modified to fit into a round cake tin too.

Step 2

Strip No.5 was used to cut a band of 'ribbon' to fit around each cake. The band was decorated with royal icing and a stencil JC6A.

Frangipani Wedding Cake

... Continued

Frangipani

Frangipani come in a variety of colours. Unless you have one to copy, it is recommended that you follow the instructions below for accuracy in shading the flower.

Step 3

Using Petal Base, lightly grease your worktop surface. Roll out paste thinly and cut five petals using the Frangipani Cutter, Set A7. Place petals on a firm piece of sponge foam. Beginning at the top of the petal , ease tool 3A down the left hand side of the petal causing it to curl slightly. Place the petals on a board and allow to partially dry flat, with the left side slightly raised from the curling process.

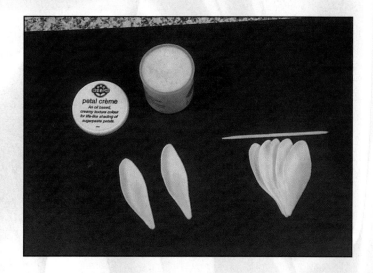

Step 4

Shade the lower part of each petal a bright yellow as illustrated. A mixture of Petal Créme and a little petal dust has been used. When the petals are holding their shape, place a little gum glue on the lower one third of the flat side of each petal. Place the next petal in position over the gummed area. The important thing to achieve whilst gluing the petals together is to make sure that the tops of the petals remain in a straight line.

Step 5

Place a little gum glue on the back of the first petal. Pick up all five petals and allow them to hang downwards. Attach the last petal to be glued to the back of the first petal. Grip all the petals together by gently easing them together in a rolling method, ensuring they are secure.

Frangipani Wedding Cake

... Continued

Step 6

Place the petals in a Handy Holder in the icing bag support position. This will effectively give you holes designed to support the frangipani. Using your fingers, open up the petals of each flower you make, allowing them to open up in different stages, eg. if you open a flower slightly it will create the appearance of a new bud. More flowers opening in different stages will create interest to your display. As soon as the flowers appear to be holding their shape, a 22 guage covered wire with a small hook on the end, may be eased into the centre.

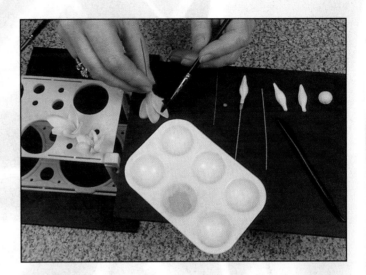

The buds are formed by rolling a ball of paste into a cylinder type shape. Using a knife, make incisions in the cylinder to represent new petals. Twist the bud for the correct effect.

When the flowers are dry, a pale pinky brown petal dust is dusted on the back of the flower. This is placed on the side of the petals that were not curled.

Step 7

Make the leaves using the largest cutter in Set A8. Cut out the leaves, not too thinly, allowing for the insertion of the wire. Place the leaves on a Petal Pad. Use Tool 10 to widen and slightly flute each leaf. Vein the leaves with veining Tool 4B.

Step 8

Dust the leaves using a dark, green petal dust. Spray them with a cooking spray to give them a sheen.

Frangipani Wedding Cake

... Continued

Step 9

Tape the flowers together in a posy style with the leaves mainly on the outside. This is how they grow.

Step 10

The side of the cake. King's Lace was made and attached to the top edge of the cake. For King's Lace see instructions on page 183.

Frangipani Wedding Cake

This cake is dedicated to Annalien, Elsie's precious daughter.

18th Birthday Celebration Cake

A 16" (40cm) scalloped oval cake tin was used for this cake. The cake was coated with almond paste and sugarpaste in the usual way. The cake board was covered separately.

Step 1

Decide on the message. You may work either directly on to the cake or use a plaque of your choice. Cut out the message using the JEM Alphabet Set and space it out before attempting to secure it. Detailed instructions to cut out lettering may be found elsewhere. Use a piece of paper with a straight edge to assist you in keeping a straight line, or cut a paper pattern to assist you in creating your message on a curve. Dampen a paint brush and lightly touch the back of the letters to attach.

Step 2

Place message on the cake or plaque. The letters are easier to place in position whilst still soft.

Step 3

Shell Border - Pipe a royal icing shell border around the cake. If you are unsure how to do this, practice first. A No.7 nozzle was used.

Apply even pressure to the bag. Remember 'squeeze' to create the bulb, 'stop squeezing' and 'pull' the tube away, leaving a tail. Begin piping the next shell on the remaining tail. Continue piping ensuring even pressure is applied.

18th Birthday Celebration Cake
... Continued

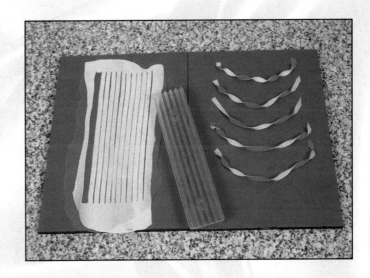

Step 4

To make the double sided twisted streamer for the side of the cake, use Strip Cutter No.3 (7mm). Two shades of paste have been used. Roll out each shade separately. Place one on top of the other - lightly roll together. Use strip cutter to cut paste. Trim ends with a knife. Twist strips to form streamer. Measure cake to work out how many scallops you will require.

Step 5

A little royal icing is used to attach the streamers to the cake.

Step 6

Make bows to neaten the streamers. Cut out bow in the size of your choice. Fold outside edges into centre. Cover join with 'bar', using gum glue to secure. Place tails under the top of bow securing with gum glue. Tails may be rigid or encouraged to have some movement. A variation of pattern used is illustrated. The narrow Strip Cutter No.1 (3mm) was used for this purpose.

18th Birthday Celebration Cake

... Continued

Step 7

Baby Daisy Sprays. For speed, use a multiple baby daisy cutter in the size of your choice. No.2 is illustrated. Dip the tops of the stamens into gum glue and ease through the centre of the daisy. Allow to dry upside down. Tape into sprays of three flowers each. Tape as many sprays together as desired.

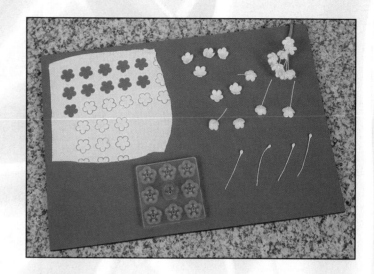

Step 8

Filler Flowers. These have been made using the same method as jasmine. Begin with a little ball of paste, smaller than a pea. Roll into a teardrop shape. Using Tool No.9, insert the 5 division side into the flower. Cut into the divisions with a small pair of scissors. Flatten each petal between your fingers. Pinch petal into shape. Insert taped wire down the middle of the trumpet. Roll between your fingers until it is neat. Leave to dry. Dust to colour of your choice. Tape into sprays.

Briar Rose

Step 9

Use dressmakers cotton for briar rose centres. Wrap cotton around two fingers about 16 times. Using very fine tinned copper wire, twist both ends of cotton firmly to prevent cotton from slipping out. Cut into two equal halves. Trim as required. Make a small paste centre using the smallest daisy centre stamp. Attach to the middle of the cotton with a little gum glue. To give the stamens body, dip the cotton centre into yellow petal créme. Separate stamens with a pin. Dip stamen tips into brown pollen.

18th Birthday Celebration Cake
... Continued

Step 10

Different sized Easy Rose Cutters have been used to create interest. When rolling out paste, leave a thick centre in the petals. This will form a base to help secure the stamens. Work the edge of the petals using tool No.10 on a Petal Pad, creating a frilly edge. Cutter 110mm is illustrated.

Step 11

A cocktail stick is used to curl the edges inwards and outwards to create a lifelike effect. Cut out a calyx suitable to the size of the flower you are making. Using a sharp knife, make slits in the calyx. JEM has a new extra large calyx with slits available for this purpose. Place the calyx in position. This helps strengthen the centre of the flower. Also it is easier to place in position at this stage. Place flower in Flower Former No.5A and support in Handy Holder. Prop up petals using small foam chips and allow to dry. Place a little gum glue at the base of stamens and ease centre into position. Remember to add the 'hip' to the dry flower.

Step 12

Rose Leaves. Roll out paste leaving a slightly thicker 'vein' down the centre into which a piece of fine taped wire may be inserted. Support the leaf between your index finger and your thumb and gently ease a 26 gauge taped wire into position. Remember to vein the top side of your leaf. A transparent veiner will allow you to correctly position the veins on the leaf. Set V1 has been used. Shade leaves with a darker green petal dust. The edges may be touched with a little red petal dust. Either spray with a cooking spray to give the leaves a sheen or pass the leaves through the steam of a kettle allowing the petal dust to dissolve, creating a soft sheen.

18th Birthday Celebration Cake

... Continued

Step 13

Assembly of sprays. Tape sprays together as desired. An informal spray is illustrated.

HINT: A base may be made for the arrangement of your flowers by using a little "platform" of fondant if you do not wish to make a bouquet or spray.

18th Birthday Celebration Cake

This cake is dedicated to my beloved daughter, Emily Jane.

Best Wishes

A 12" (30cm) round cake was used for this design. The cake board was 15" (38cm). Both the cake and the board were covered simultaneously in sugarpaste (rolled fondant) that was shaded with peach paste colouring.

Step 1

The Hollow Oval side cutter was used for the top and the base of the cake. Lightly grease worktop surface with a little Petal Base. Roll out paste and cut out as many hollow ovals as required for the circumference of the cake. Place these over a right angled box, or similar, to dry. An ice cream box has been used in the photograph. Leave to dry.

Step 2

The sides of the cake have been stencilled in coloured royal icing. Use a little sellotape or a sticky label and block out the contrasting section of the stencil. This will enable you to make the leaves green and the flowers a colour of your choice. Decide how many stencils to place on the side of your cake. Position the stencil and, using a little royal icing on a spatula, fill in one of the colours. Leave to dry. Remove blocked out areas and block remaining areas and repeat exercise. Note: The stencilling was done on the actual cake and not separately as indicated in the photograph.

Step 3

Tiny filler flowers were cut out using the Eight Petal Daisy Wheel. These were placed on a Petal Pad and indented using the Daisy Point Tool No.16B. The little flowers were then attached to the stencilled picture to give a 3-D dimension to the side of the cake.

Best Wishes

... Continued

Step 4

Stephanotis was made as a filler flower. The finger flower method was used together with Tool 9. Make a tiny ball slightly smaller than a pea. Shape this into a teardrop. Press the five division side of Tool 9 into the top of the teardrop to make an impression. Using your fingers, flatten each section and then pinch the ends of the petals to give the flower shape. Open the throat of the flower using Tool 2B. Ensure that the back of your flower is long and narrow with a slight bump at the base. Insert a taped wire (gauge 26) into the middle of the flower. Pull this down into the throat of the flower so that it is just visible.

Step 5

The calyx was cut out using the Five Petal Daisy Wheel. Attach to the base of the flower with a little gum glue. Note the shape of the bud.

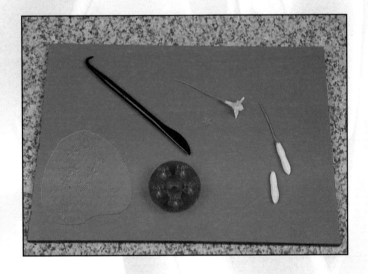

Step 6

The side of the cake.

197

Best Wishes

... Continued

Step 7
The briar roses. Instructions for the briar rose appear on page 192.

HINT: Wire may be omitted in the structure of flowers or foliage if preferred.

Best Wishes

Best Wishes

This cake is dedicated to my loyal staff at JEM Cutters South Africa, who have assisted me by working hard and faithfully.

Magnolia Wedding Cake

Three six petal cake tins were used for this cake. The measurements were 7" (18cm), 9" (23cm) and 11" (28cm) respectively. The cake boards were specially made and measured 9" (23cm), 12" (30cm) and 16" (40cm) respectively. All the cakes were covered in cream sugarpaste (rolled fondant) separately on spare cake boards that were covered with wax paper to protect the cake boards. The cake boards were covered in sugarpaste and allowed to dry for at least 48 hours. The edges of the cake board were covered in a burgundy ribbon the same shade that will be used for the shading of the flowers. A royal icing shell border using a No.7 nozzle was piped around the base of the cakes to secure the cakes to the cake boards.

Step 1

The decoration around the edge of the cake board was made from the S-Heart Scroll side cutter. These were cut out on a surface lightly greased with Petal Base. They were allowed to partially dry. They were then interlocked into each other and placed around the side of the cake board whilst they were still soft. (See Step 3).

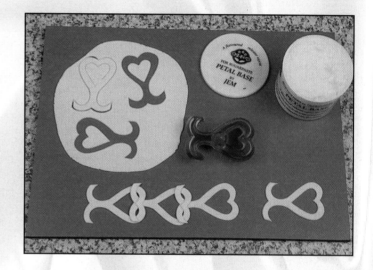

Step 2

The same heart scroll cutter was used to cut out hollow hearts. The base was trimmed. Small hearts in the same shade of Burgundy paste were cut out using a heart cutter from Set A20. These were placed in the centre of each petal curve on the cakes.

HINT: Work paste through at least once a week if not in use. This will prolong its 'life'.

Magnolia Wedding Cake

... Continued

Step 3

The heart scroll chain was attached to the base of the cake board using a little royal icing. The protruding edge around the side of each cake makes an unusual border for a cake.

Magnolia

Step 4

Make the cotton centres by wrapping sewing cotton around two fingers at least 32 times to give you a full centre. Grip firmly with fine tinned copper wire on two sides of the circle ensuring that the cotton will not slip out. Cut the cotton in half with a small pair of sharp scissors to give you two centres. Ready made cotton stamens are available from JEM. Trim excess length.

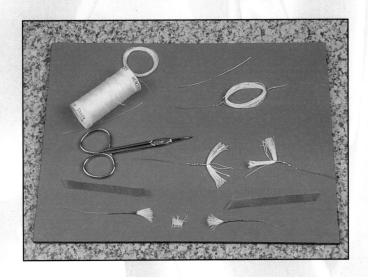

Step 5

To give the stamens 'body', mix two shades of Petal Créme together. Grape Juice and Red Velvet have been used. Apply the créme thoroughly to the stamens. Wipe off excess on a piece of paper towel and separate the stamens. Three stamen clusters are required for each flower.

Magnolia Wedding Cake

... Continued

Step 6

Roll out a small ball of paste in Burgundy, slightly larger than a pea. Shape this onto a 20 guage taped wire to form a cone about 15mm long. Using a small, sharp pair of scissors, cut numerous tiny stamens into the tip, working down evenly from the top around the centre. Paint the tip of each of these stamens with white petal créme. Tape three cotton centres evenly around the centre.

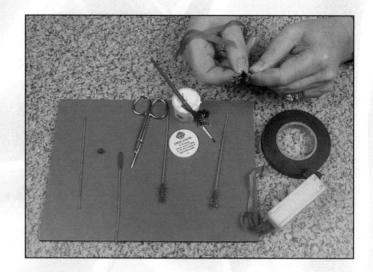

Step 7

Lightly grease your worktop surface with Petal Base. Roll out paste, allowing for the insertion of wire at the base of each petal. Cut out the petals. The petals for this flower are waxy in appearance and therefore are not required to be paper thin. Place the petals on a Petal Pad and slightly soften the edges with Tool 10. Using the ball tool, slightly increase the length of the petal at the top rounded part of each petal. Pinch a small crease into the top back of each petal.

Step 8

Vein each petal with a corn veiner, Set V5. Make the several prominent veins found in the petals, by lightly pressing Tool 4B into each petal, pulling it down from the top to the base of the petal. Dry over petal former 1A.

Magnolia Wedding Cake
... Continued

Step 9
Dust the dry petals with petal dust ensuring that you leave the tips of the petals white. Work over a receptacle to avoid wasting excess dust.

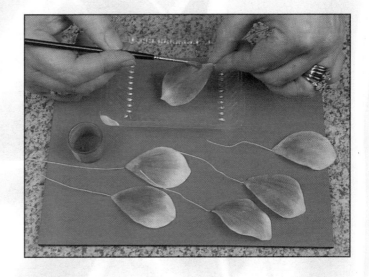

Step 10
Tape three petals to the centre using brown tape. Place the next three petals in between the first row of petals. Position the petals so that they form flowers in different stages from half open to fully open.

Step 11
Cut out leaves using various sizes taken from the water lily Set A8. Remember to allow for the insertion of taped wire, guage 25. The leaves must be in a light, bright green, representing new leaves. This particular magnolia begins to flower when there are a few new leaves beginning to appear on the tree. When the leaves are dry, use brown tape to tape the flowers into a spray, creating woody stems. Vein the leaves using Tool 4B.

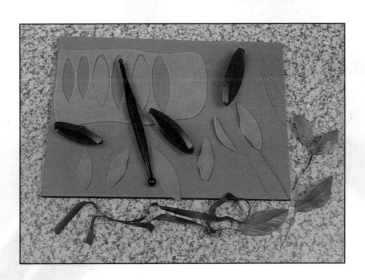

Magnolia Wedding Cake

A split level tiered stand has been used for this cake.

Out of Africa

An 8" (20cm) square cake tin and a 12" (30cm) cake board was used for this cake. An additional cake board 15" (38cm) square was used to display the cake. The cake and the top board were covered simultaneously in sugarpaste (rolled fondant). The extra display board was also covered in white sugarpaste. The edges of the cake board were covered in black ribbon.

The colours used for the Ndebele work featured on this cake were black, mauve, orange, yellow, blue and red. Black strips of paste were cut out and placed on the centre of each board around the cake, to add interest. Strip No.2 and 3 were used for this purpose.

Step 1

The card was made using J4-7. This was rolled out on a lightly greased worktop surface and cut out of blue paste and allowed to dry. Allow cards to dry on flat sponge foam. This allows the air to circulate thereby assisting in the drying process. The lettering and patterns were cut out and placed in position on the dry card whilst they were still soft. Strip No.2 was used to decorate the card. Cutter No.K from the geometrical quilting patch designs was used for the decoration on the card. The lettering was made using the JEM Alphabet set.

Step 2

The decorations on the cake were cut out using Cutter J and K from the Quilting Patch Designs. A strip in blue paste was cut out using Strip No.4 as a base to form the top pattern of the cake. This also appears on the top cake board forming a base border.

Out of Africa

... Continued

Step 3

Additional patterns and colours are illustrated showing a rose petal cutter which has been cut in half to form a semi circle. The square Cutter A is used to represent a little Ndebele hut.

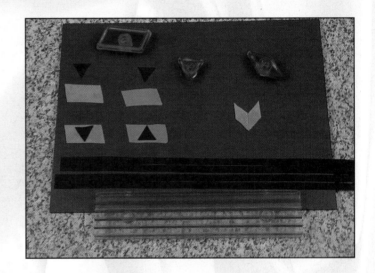

Step 4

The slanted pattern on the blue band was made using Cutter F as a background.

Step 5

A close-up of this cake. A No.1 Strip cutter was used on the top of the cake to make the black strips dividing the cake into sections.

Out of Africa

This cake is dedicated to my elder brother, Martin McLachlan, for whom I care deeply.

A Very Happy Christmas

A Very simple cake for a beginner to attempt.
A 10" (25cm) hexagonal cake tin was used for this cake. The cake was placed on a 14" (35cm) cake board. The fondant was coloured cream and the cake and the board were covered simultaneously.

Step 1

Lightly grease your worktop surface with Petal Base. Roll out different coloured modelling paste and cut out the parcels using cutter J5-4. Move the cutter into the paste at different right angles creating a variety of different sized parcels. The cutter will assist you by giving the parcels square corners. Decorate the individual parcels using a No. 1 tube and coloured royal icing to create parcel bows. The parcels may be decorated immediately and carefully attached to the cake whilst still soft. Use Tool No.13 to pick up the parcels to avoid distorting them. Arrange the parcels as desired around the base of the cake.

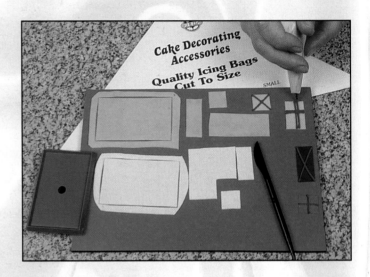

Step 2

Lightly grease your worktop surface with Petal Base. Roll out your paste thin enough to give the lettering shape without it sticking in the cutters. Cut out the message "A VERY HAPPY CHRISTMAS" in upper case lettering. If paste should stick in the odd letter, use a pin or other sharp object to lift a corner of the letter to release it. Lettering should remain on your worktop surface. Lettering is easier to position whilst still soft.

Using Strip No.1, cut out paste in a colour of your choice to create streamers. Twist the strips of paste around a narrow dowel stick or a paint brush. As soon as paste holds the curve of the dowel, ease the paste off and arrange on the side of the cake and the base of the Christmas tree as desired. The base of the Christmas tree was made by using a cutter from Set J5-6. This shape was trimmed to size.

A Very Happy Christmas
... Continued

Step 3

Cut out a number of different miniature Christmas shapes in a variety of colours, sufficient to create rows in between the message. These may be placed on the cake whilst still damp. If necessary, a damp paint brush could be used to ensure they remain in place on the cake.

COVERING CAKES WITH SUGARPASTE (ROLLED FONDANT)

1. Make sure the cake is in the centre of the board and that the board is the correct size.
2. Dampen the almond covering on the cake with a clean pastry brush and a little boiled water.
3. Knead the sugarpaste very well before you begin. It should absorb enough 'body heat' to make it soft and pliable before you start.
4. Roll out sugarpaste on a worktop surface that has been lightly dusted with sieved icing sugar.
5. Try to keep the sugarpaste in the same shape as the cake eg. round for a round cake or square for a square cake.
6. Roll out sugarpaste evenly. It should be about $1/2$" (10mm) thick, but may be less.
7. Measure the size of the cakes against the size of the rolled out fondant. A piece of string is useful for this purpose. Take into consideration whether you wish to cover only the cake or if you plan to include the cake board.
8. Pick up the sugarpaste either by using two 'lifters' (pieces of kitchen panelite or similar) or wrap the sugarpaste around your roller. Place the sugarpaste over the centre of the cake and quickly withdraw either the lifters or the roller.
9. Prick any air bubbles with a hat pin by easing the pin into the bubble at an angle. Smooth over the surface.
10. If you are working on a square cake, or a cake that has corners, begin by lightly pressing the sugarpaste against the corners. Gently ease the sugarpaste against the rest of the cake. A round cake is easier to cover.
11. Having successfully covered the cake, use a *pair* of JEM smoothers to remove any trace of finger marks. This will create a professional finish.
12. Use a soft cloth to 'polish' the cake. This effectively removes all traces of icing sugar and will give the surface a soft sheen.
13. If you plan to leave the cake board plain, place the cake on a piece of wax paper, making sure that you will be able to remove the paper after covering the cake. This will keep the board clean.

Megan's Christening Cake

A 11" (28cm) round cake tin was used for this cake. The cake was coated in the normal way in white sugarpaste (rolled fondant).

Step 1

Lightly grease surface with Petal Base. The edge used to trim the base of the cake was made by placing the oval frieze cutter and a medium strip cutter together on a piece of rolled out flower paste. This created an interesting edge on one side and a straight edge on the other side.

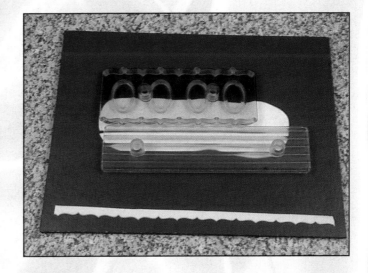

Step 2

A single strip was cut out long enough to go around the entire cake. This was attached to the cake with a little water.

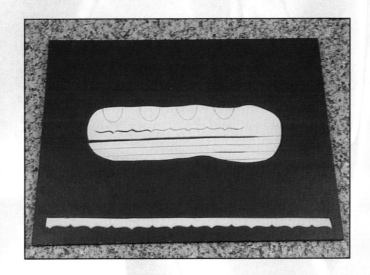

Step 3

Roll out paste on worktop surface lightly greased with Petal Base. Using the Oval Frieze cutter, cut out seven sections. Remove centres. Trim edges.

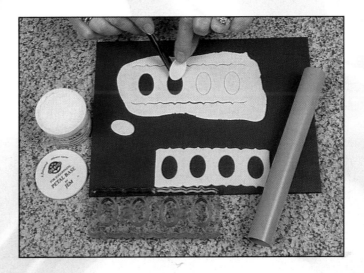

Megan's Christening Cake

... Continued

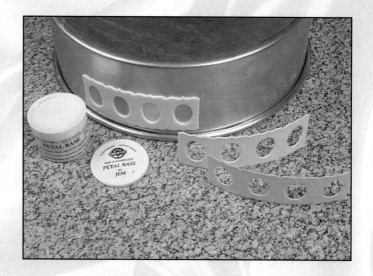

Step 4

Lightly grease the outside of the tin used for the cake, and place the sections on the tin and allow to dry completely. When the sections are dry, they will be able to stand up.

Step 5

Make the blossom, (see instructions on page 51).

Tape several blossoms and leaves together using brown tape. Place the blossom through the oval opening and attach the blossom sprays to the back of the oval frieze section with a tiny ball of sugarpaste. Leave to dry. *Evenly space the sections around the cake board. Attach the sections to the cake board with a little royal icing.*

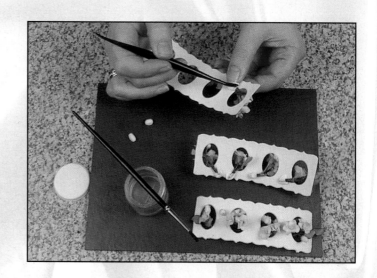

Step 6

A close-up of the frieze.

Megan's Christening Cake

... Continued

Step 7

Roll out flower paste and using a medium strip cutter, cut out strips in a contrasting colour for ribbon insertion. Trim with Tool 13A into even sections that fit over a narrow rod. Leave to dry completely.

Baby's Bib

Step 8

Roll out flower paste not too thinly. Using Cutter P3, cut out the bib. Cutter J4-6 will cut out the neck, creating an inverted scallop for the bib.

Step 9

Using the pair of bird cutters, Set J6-9, cut out and remove the white birds. Using Tool No.4A, lightly flute the edges of the bib. Tool No.18 was used for the insertion of the paste ribbon into the bib. Measure and space the insertions on the bib evenly. Tool No.16A was used to make the pattern around the neck.

Megan's Christening Cake

... Continued

Step 10

In a contrasting colour, cut out the birds again, and replace them into the bib. Using the medium strip cutter, No.2, cut out strips that may be used to tie a bow for the bib.

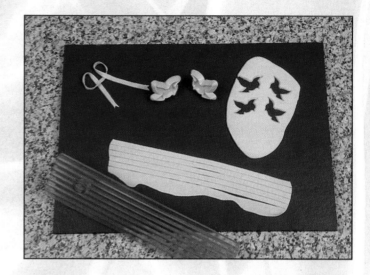

Step 11

Pipe on the name in royal icing and link the birds with a piped ribbon on the bib using a No.1 tube. When the bib is dry, lightly dust with a little lustre.

HINT: Work in a good light.   It is preferable to shade petals, foliage etc., in the daylight.

Megan's Christening Cake

This cake is dedicated to my niece, Megan McLachlan.

Bibs

Numerous variations are possible when making babies' bibs.

Step 1

A display of various equipment that could be used when making bibs includes JEM Doily cutters, round disc cutters, Carnation Plaque cutter, Circle Cutter J4-15 and Baby Bib Cutter J6-4 and small scalloped circle J5-7 for neckline. Stencils to decorate small bibs are useful, as well as small daisy cutters and tiny bows. Tweezers could be used to make pleats. Frilling tools used on the edges will soften the appearance of the bib.

Step 2

Life-size bibs may be made using the following cutters. P3 - scalloped circle and P2 the fancy oval. To create the inverted scalloped neckline, Cutter J4-6 has been used. Cutter J4-15 is a plain circle. Cutter J4-9 is the smaller version of the fancy oval cutter. The larger bibs could be decorated with little cutout animals, for example ducks and lambs, as well as stencils. Different tools could create various effects to the edges of the bibs. The bibs could be dusted with lustre dust to create a satin appearance. Lustre may be applied to wet paste.

HINT: The impression of the tool you are using should not remain visible on the surface of your work.

Bibs

A selection of bibs using various cutters.

Murray's Christening Cake

A 10" (25cm) hexagonal tin was used for this cake. The cake board measures 15" (38cm). The cake and the board were covered simultaneously in blue rolled fondant.

Step 1

A number of Double Square Side Cutters were cut out to form a pattern on this cake. The paste was rolled out on a surface lightly greased with Petal Base. Remove the inside square and the surrounding paste then simply stretch the pattern to form a triangular pattern.

The pieces were placed on the cake whilst they were still soft. A little water was used to attach them to the cake surface.

Step 2

Three different baby daisies were cut out in different shades to form a pattern on the double squares on the cake. These were attached to the cake with a little gum glue.

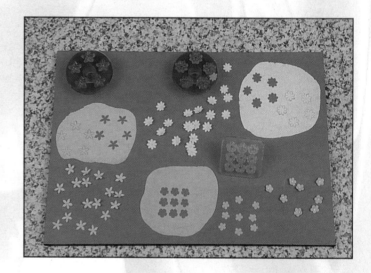

Step 3

The side of the cake

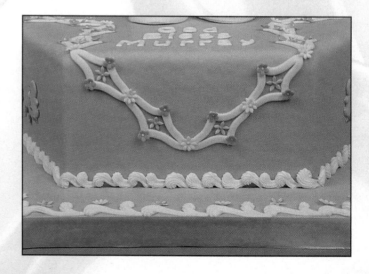

Murray's Christening Cake
... Continued

Felicia
Step 4
To mix the correct colour for the Felicia, mix 3 parts violet to one part of royal blue. Use taped wire, gauge 28, for these flowers.

The blue daisy, (Felicia) was made using size 1, 2 and 3 of the Six Petal Daisy Cutters. Roll a tiny piece of paste, about the size of a pea, into a ball. Shape into a cone and then flatten the edges making a 'Mexican hat'. *Hold the cutter in your hand and place the 'Mexican hat' over the middle of the cutter. Using your fingers apply even pressure on the cutter, causing the petals to be cut out. Using Tool 4A, flatten the petals, slightly open the throat of the flower, and then slit each petal into two, using Tool 13A.*

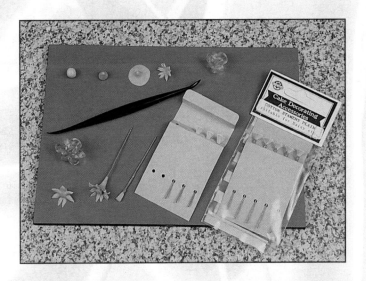

Ready made yellow cotton centres have been used in this flower. Place a little gum glue into the middle of the flower and ease the wired stamens through the centre of the flower.

The calyx was made using Cutter B36 (not illustrated), the second smallest cutter in Set B11. This was rolled out flat and attached to the back of the flower.

Step 5
Cut out several leaves in different sizes for each daisy. Cutters taken from Set B21 make very useful leaves. In this case, the leaf was cut twice moving the cutter down, thereby creating a smaller leaf. The leaves were veined with a veiner from Set V2.

The leaves were taped together in varying sizes to form a circle. They were dusted with a dark green petal dust and sprayed with a cooking spray to give them a sheen.

Murray's Christening Cake

God Bless Murray

This cake is dedicated to my father, Murray McLachlan, who has always been the gentleman in my life.

Bootees

Step 1

On a lightly greased surface, roll out flower paste. Cut out the toe of the bootee. If desired, make an impression with another cutter. In this case, an oval scalloped cutter was used from Set J5-7. Allow this to 'skin dry'.

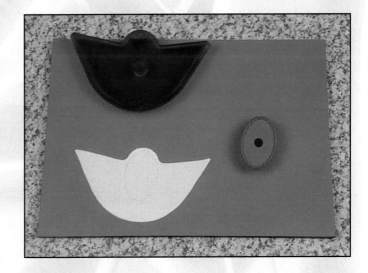

Step 2

Cut out the heel of the bootee using paste the same thickness as the paste used for the toe. Allow to 'skin dry'.

Cut out the sole of the bootee using paste that is as thick as the cutter allows. Place the sole on a piece of wax paper. This will assist you in turning the bootee around as you assemble it.

Note: The sole of the bootee has 'toe' engraved on it. This will assist you in placing the top of the bootee in the correct position.

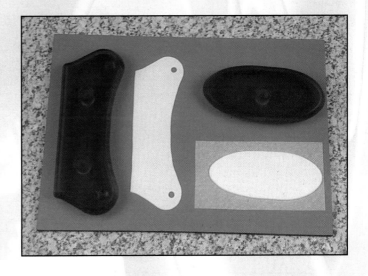

Step 3

Using a little gum glue around the toe of the sole, place the 'skin dried' top toe of the bootee in position. Support with a little 'cloud drift'.

Place a little gum glue on the heel of the sole and attach the heel, ensuring that it joins the toe of the bootee.

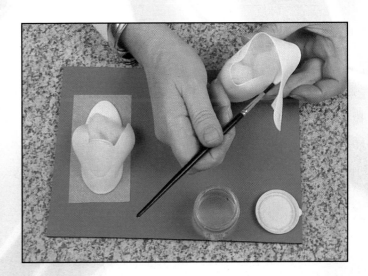

Bootees

... Continued

Step 4

To make the laces, use the narrow strip cutter No.1. Thread the laces through the bootee as desired.

Little ducks, Set J6-11 have been used to decorate the bootee. They were cut out of yellow paste and their beaks and feet were shaded with Sunburst Orange Petal Créme.

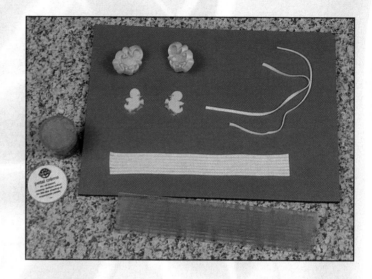

Step 5

Back and front of bootees.

Note: The base of the bootees were trimmed with a medium strip cutter, No.2. Use a dress maker's wheel to create stitches on the strip.

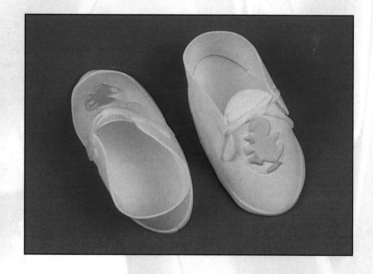

Step 6

Finished bootees.

Bootees

... Continued

Step 7

Some more suggestions for the front of the life-size bootee. Small oval and round scalloped cutters are found in Set J5-7. The lambs, ducks, rabbits and birds are found in Sets J6-10, J6-11, J6-6 and J6-9 respectively.The daisy wheel cutters are also useful in adding interest to the front of the bootees.

Step 8

Other ideas include the use of the scalloped circle J4-5, Miniature hearts and Miniature Bows found in the Wedding Miniature set, as well as the dogs and swans found in Sets 8 and J6-7 respectively. The short friller, Tool 15A was used to frill the edges of the circle. The bootees may be dusted with lustre dust to give them a satin sheen.

Step 9

This photo illustrates the JEM Medium Bootee and the steps to construct it. The JEM miniature bootee may be found in Set A19. A stripfor the strap will have to be cut out freehand, or by using Strip No.1

Bootees

A selection of bootees in various sizes.

Spring Wedding Cake

This cake was designed to fit an 11" (28cm) diameter antique wedding cake stand. The measurements of the cakes used are as folows:

Bottom tier   Cake 10" (25 cm)   Cake board 11" (28cm)
Middle tier   Cake 9" (23cm)   Cake board 10" (25cm)
Top tier   Cake 6" (15 cm)   Cake board 8" (20cm)

Cover the cake in the usual way and pipe a shell border around cakes.

Cotton Centres

Step 1

Cotton Centres - make cotton centres for both the briar rose and the daisies. Wind cotton around your index finger about 15 times. Twist very fine wire, gripping the cotton firmly on two sides of the circle. Cut the cotton in half - this will give you two centres. Tape each centre onto a firmer wire (gauge 25). Trim cotton to desired length.

Dip the cotton into Petal Créme to give the stamens body and to create a pollen effect for the daisy. The briar rose centres should also be dipped into a light brown "pollen" mixture.

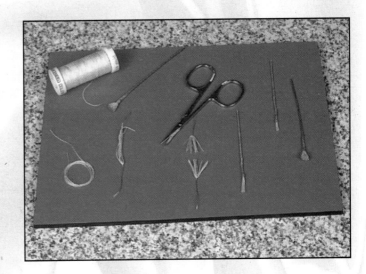

Step 2

The Briar Rose - lightly grease your worktop surface with a little JEM Petal Base. Roll out your modelling paste thinly and cut out petals for the briar rose, using JEM Easy Rose Cutter size 50mm.

Use a blend of Petal Créme to colour the briar rose. Shade the centre of the briar rose using Sunshine Yellow (No.1) and the edges with Débutante Pink (No.7). The créme may be applied with the tip of your finger.

Spring Wedding Cake

... Continued

Step 3

Place the petal on a Petal Pad and lightly frill the petals with a ball tool, JEM Tool 10. Using a cocktail stick, curl the petals both inwards and outwards.

Step 4

Cut out a calyx using JEM calyx No.73. Place the calyx at the back of the wet petals and place the flower in JEM flower former No.2A for small cupped flower.

Step 5

Clip the flower former cups into the Handy Holder stand. Use flower former No.5A for a larger open briar rose. Sponge chips are useful to give your petals form. Apply a little gum glue to the base of the cotton stamens and insert stamens into the centre of your flower. When the flower is dry, remove from stand and, using a tiny piece of green paste, shape and attach a "hip" to the rose. This will neaten wend strengthen the flower.

Spring Wedding Cake
... Continued

Step 6

Daisies - rub a little JEM Petal Base on your board and using JEM B34 cut out two rows of petals to make a daisy. Using JEM Tool 12, roll each petal on a petal pad to create a veined effect. JEM B35 will make a slightly smaller daisy. Use B36 for the calyx for both daisies. Place one row of petals in between the next row of petals. Attach the calyx to the wet petals.

Step 7

Place the daisy petals into JEM flower former 2B. Using JEM Tool No.10, press into the centre of the daisy to "cup" the flower. Apply a little gum glue to the base of the cotton stamens and insert through the centre of the daisy. When the daisies are dry, you may attach a second calyx to the flower to neaten and strengthen it.

Easy Rose

Step 8

Easy Rose - to make a quick rose, you need a dry centre cone on a 24 gauge wire. If you are making a small rose, you will need two layers of petals using JEM Easy Rose Cutter size 80mm. A larger rose will have a third row of petals using a 90mm cutter. Apply a little Petal Base to the worktop surface and roll out the petals in the usual way, ensuring the petals are thin enough. Shade the petals with petal créme. Leave the centre of the petals white. Shade the petal yellow, tipping the edges with pink. Place the largest petal on a Petal Pad and soften the edges with Tool 10. Curl the petals using a cocktail stick away from the centre of the petals. Allow to partially dry. The middle row should be worked in the same manner. Do not curl the small inside petals.

Spring Wedding Cake
... Continued

Step 9

The Easy Rose cutters have numbers marked on each petal to assist the decorator in the building up of a rose. Place the cone in the centre of the small petals. Look at your cutter and decide which petal will be the first petal to attach to the cone, then pick up petal No. 2,3,4 and 5. You will find that what you are actually doing is picking up one petal, missing a petal and picking up the next petal to wrap around the cone. In the same manner, attach the next row of petals. Add a third row for the larger rose.

When the roses are dry, cut out a calyx and attach to the back of the flower. Remember to add a tiny "hip" to neaten the flower.

Step 10

To make a bud - the cone could be the same size as for the Easy Rose. Cut out two or three single petals using JEM No.28. Shade the petals using the petal créme, attach to the cone. Add a calyx and "hip" to neaten.

Step 11

Leaves - rose leaves set L10 have been used in the spray. Remember to leave a slight ridge down the centre of your leaf when rolling out your paste for the insertion of the wire. When taping the leaves together, the larger leaf goes at the top of the sprig. These leaves were made using a green paste and have been shaded using the petal créme. Valley Green (No.14) and Green Trees (No.15) for the leaf. The edges were tipped with Red Roses (No.5), using a firm brush with a flat base.

Spring Wedding Cake
... Continued

Step 12

Tape your spray of flowers together. Begin with a small leaf and bud, working up gradually until the spray fills out on the sides. Make both sides of the spray and simply slip the one into the other creating a balanced effect. Save your largest flower for your focal point.

Step 13

Side of Cake - cut out a frill using JEM F3B and using JEM F1A, cut into the top of frill F3B, creating an unusual effect.

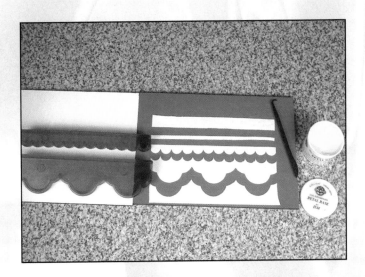

Step 14

Attach frills to the cakes by brushing a little water on the frill. Remember to leave an equal distance between the frills.

Spring Wedding Cake
... Continued

Step 15

Cut out baby daisies, using JEM Daisy Wheel Cutter - 8 petal daisy. Cup these daisies using Daisy Point Tool No.16B. Attach these to the centre of the frills on the side of the cake.

Step 16

Cut out Miniature Bells - press Tool 4B lightly into the bells. This will give the bells shape. Tip the edges of the bells silver. Attach the bells to each scallop of the frill.

HINT: Make your own pollen by using a mixture of maize meal and petal dust. If you wish to have a shimmering effect, use caster sugar mixed with a little petal dust.

Spring Wedding Cake

Patchwork for Dad

A 7 1/2" (19cm) hexagonal cake tin was used for this cake. The board measured 10" (25cm). The cake was positioned at the back of a larger cake board that measured 14" (36cm). The cake and the first board were covered in a dark chocolate brown sugarpaste (rolled fondant). The larger board was covered in beige. Strip No.1 was used for the side of the cake.

Step 1

Roll out paste and texture it with a smoking roller. Cut out numerous shapes using the Quilting Patch Cutter No.C. As you work, keep the shapes under cling wrap to prevent them drying out.

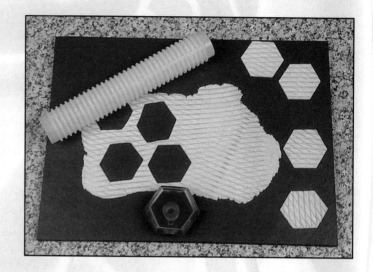

Step 2

Cut out more shapes using the same cutter, but introduce a different coloured paste and something else to texture the paste. Plastic shower glass has been used. The five petal daisy wheel cutter has also been used to introduce different coloured flowers to add interest to the material effect needed for the patchwork theme. Place the damp shapes on the cake, forming the desired pattern. Cutter J4-5 was used to cut out the scalloped circles that were cut in half to form an edge to both boards.

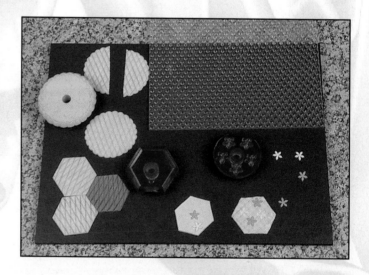

HINT: Keep your flower paste sealed in a plastic bag placed in a placed container with a lid. Each colour should be in a separate bag.

Step 3

The scroll card Set J4-12 was used for the name. Use a cocktail stick to curl the edges backwards and forwards on the scroll.

Step 4

A few more ideas for patterns using the Quilting Patch Designs.

Patchwork for Dad

Patchwork for Dad

This cake is dedicated to my Dad, Murray McLachlan, and to my children's Dad, Neil Maytham.

Joining of the Clans

A 10" (25cm) square tin was used for this cake. The cake was placed across the corners on a 16" (40cm) square board. The cake and the board were covered separately in beige sugarpaste (rolled fondant). The cake was placed on an additional 18" (45cm) square cake board for aesthetic purposes. The edge of this board was covered in dark brown sugarpaste.

Daisies Galore

Step 1

A variety of daisies were made for this cake. Centres in different colours and sizes were made using the JEM Daisy Centre Stamps. Covered wires gauge 22 and 25 were used for the different flowers. A flat hook was made at the end of each wire. This was eased into the different centres and allowed to dry.

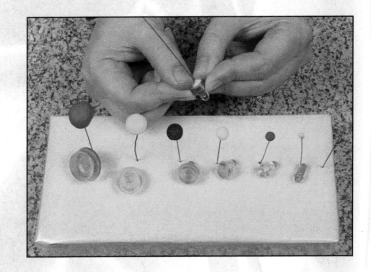

Step 2

Lightly grease worktop surface with Petal Base. Roll out white paste and, using a small chrysanthemum / daisy cutter taken from Set B11, cut out numerous petals. Press Tool 4A into each petal to create a veinal impression.

HINT: If paste should stick in a cutter, use a pin to lift out the petal or foliage.

Step 3

Attach two layers to a small daisy centre encouraging the petals to almost cover the centre. This will create a half open effect for a small daisy. The calyx was made from the Eight Petal Daisy Wheel Cutter.

Step 4

Several sizes taken from Set B11 are illustrated. Tool No.13A has been used to split each petal in half. Tool 12 has been rolled backwards and forwards on each petal causing it to be veined and widened at the same time. The petals may be shaded in a variety of colours at this stage. Attach petals to a centre by beginning with the smallest petals first. Continue to build up the daisy adding the larger petals last. Two layers of the smaller cutters should be used for the calyx.

Step 5

Different sized daisy petals are illustrated here. The petals have been left whole. Tool 12 has been used to vein and flute the individual petals.

Step 6

The daisies illustrated are supported in the Handy Holder on flower formers 3B and 5A respectively. Individual petals have been supported with small pieces of sponge foam to give movement to the petals. Several different daisies are illustrated.

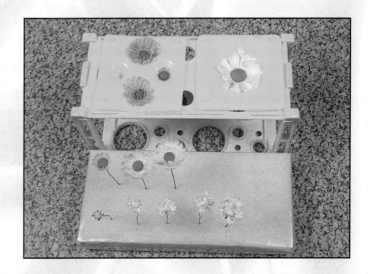

Step 7

The large Eight Petal Daisy has been used for some of the daisies. These petals may be split if desired or remain as individual petals. Tool 12 is excellent for veining each petal and giving it shape. Use the smaller daisy cutters in Set B11 for the calyx.

Step 8

Daisies made with ready made cotton stamens are illustrated. Petals are made in the same manner but it is suggested that slightly thicker daisy centres will assist in supporting the cotton centres. Gum glue is placed at the base of the cotton stamens and pulled through the middles of the daisies. Make a calyx using the small cutters in Set B11.

Joining of the Clans
... Continued

Step 9

A variety of daisy leaves may be used. Cutters taken from set L4B and L6C have been used in the daisy sprays. Provision was made for the insertion of taped wire by not rolling out the stem of the leaf too thinly. The leaves may be veined with Tool 4B. If you use different cutters, change the shading of the leaves to enhance the effect.

Step 10

A wire coat hanger was straightened. This was then covered in florist tape and twisted around a cylinder to form a spiral.

Step 11

Tape the various daisies into individual sprays. Then beginning at the tip of the spiral, carefully tape the individual sprays into position. A fairly heavy piece of sugarpaste was cut out using a cookie cutter to give the spiral ballast. See the Cosmos Wedding Cake.

Joining of the Clans
... Continued

Step 12

The badges on the cake were cut out using Set J5-15. Strip No.1 was used to create the different shields.

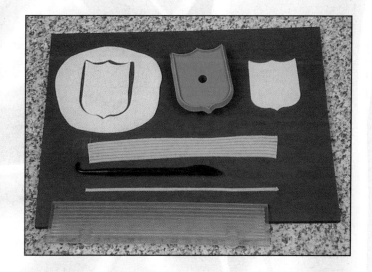

Step 13

Heraldry. Different cutters that could be used in creating shields are the cross found in Set A18, the miniature reindeer found in the Miniature Christmas Set No.1 and punctuation marks found in the JEM alphabet set. King's Lace and the snowdrop cutter can be found in Set B16.

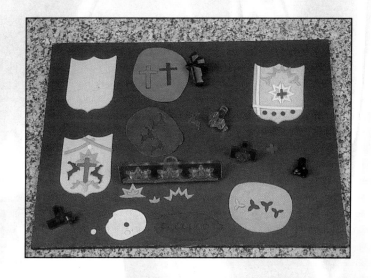

Step 14

More ideas for heraldry, using Strip No.2, the miniature Christmas tree and cutter found in the JEM geometrical quilting patch designs.

Joining of the Clans

... Continued

Step 15

The banner was cut out using Strip No.4. This was allowed to partially dry so that it would be able to stand up on its side. The message was cut out from the JEM Alphabet Set and placed in position using a damp paint brush.

Step 16

A close-up of the daisies.

This cake is dedicated to my husband Neil, with love.

Quilling

Quilling is a paper craft used to make various types of decoration in pictures and on cards. Narrow strips of coloured paper, sometimes in varying widths, are used to roll into coils and scrolls. Tightly rolled coils are sometimes used. Other coils are encouraged to unravel slightly and are shaped between the fingers into numerous patterns. These different shapes are then used to build up patterns and pictures. For more ideas, it is recommended that you obtain a book on quilling.

This art form is easily adapted to sugarcraft.

Step 1

Lightly grease your worktop surface with Petal Base. Roll out various coloured pastes and, using Strip No.1, cut out a number of strips. Cover the strips with cling wrap to keep them soft until they are required. The strips need to be pliable, but not too soft, when used. Separate a single strip. Hook the strip into the quilling tool, Tool 11. Hold the tool in an upright position and form a coil. If you require a tight coil, it will be necessary to place a little glue in the centre of the coil to keep it tightly closed. To form a pattern in the coil, use a cocktail stick to gently encourage the strip to unravel. Use a damp pant brush or a little gum glue to secure the outside edge to the back of the scroll. Form the pattern you require by shaping the coil between your fingers whilst it is still on the board.

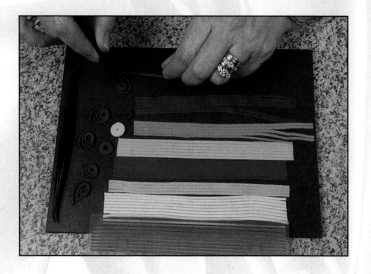

Step 2

Choose a pattern of your choice. Place the pattern on a flat surface, (polystyrene has been used) and cover this with a sheet of wax wrap. Secure the wax wrap with pins. Work with dressmaker's pins to assist you in holding the soft coils in position whilst they dry on the pattern. It will be necessary to glue the coils together, with a little gum glue, where they touch each other.

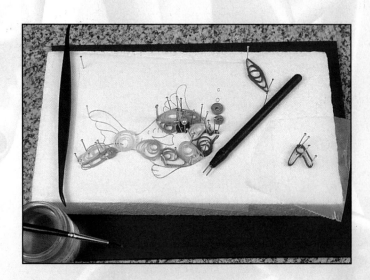

Quilling
... Continued

Step 3
Roll out paste about 2mm thick and cut out a Plaque Stand. Dry this over a right angle so that it will stand upright when it is dry.

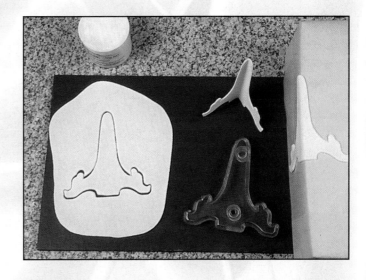

Step 4
Prepared backgrounds, using various plaques, have been made ahead of time. When the quilling is dry, apply a little gum glue to the picture and place it in position on the selected plaque.

HINT: If you wish to create a "drop of water" effect on your work, simply dissolve a little clear gelatin and carefully release a single drop onto the petal etc.

Quilling

A few ideas of simple quiling in paste. Plaque P1, three sizes of the Doily Cutters and a Round Disc Cutter are illustrated.

This is dedicated to my precious son and special friend, Michael Neil.

The Magic of Christmas

A 9" (23cm) round cake was baked for this cake. It was placed on a 15" (38cm) cake board to allow for the curved church windows that form part of the decoration on this cake. The cake and the board were covered simultaneously in white sugarpaste (rolled fondant). The cake was then placed on another cake board 18" (45cm) in diameter. The edge of this board was covered with red sugarpaste. The tartan ribbons around the edge of the cake boards add colour to the cake.

Step 1

On a lightly greased worktop surface roll out paste about 1mm thick and cut out as many window frieze strips as you will need. Trim the edges with a knife. Allow the strips to air dry before removing the centres from the windows. At this stage place them on a cylinder shape that has been covered in wax paper and leave to dry. Measure the cake to ensure the windows are spaced evenly around the cake. Use a little royal icing to secure the windows to the cake board.

Step 2

Cut out ten miniature reindeer in brown paste. This cutter is found in the Miniature Cutter Set No.1. Using the miniature Christmas sleigh cutter taken from the Miniature Christmas Set No.3, cut out the sleigh in red paste. Cut out the miniature teddy bear found in the same set. Remove the teddy bear's legs and his right ear using Tool 13A. By painting his clothes red and his beard white, this will enable you to create a little Father Christmas to sit in the sleigh.

HINT: If you live in humid conditions, a cupboard with an electric light bulb fitted in the base is an exellent way to store and preserve flowers or foliage. The cupboard should have small vent holes at the top to allow the hot air to escape.

The Magic of Christmas
... Continued

Step 3

The tree in the Christmas scene is a daisy leaf taken from Set L6C. The miniature choir boys were made from the miniature angel cutter found in the Christmas miniature Set No.3. Simply cut off the wings and paint the robe red to make a choir boy.

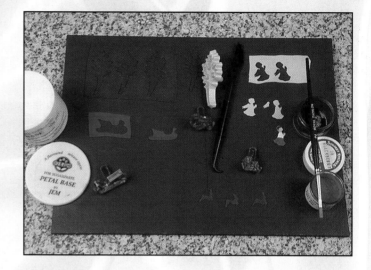

Step 4

The moon was made from the large daisy centre stamp. The star of Bethlehem was taken from the Miniature Christmas Set 1. The house and the church are both Patchwork Cutters. Detailed instructions on how to create these items may be found in Marion Frost's books.

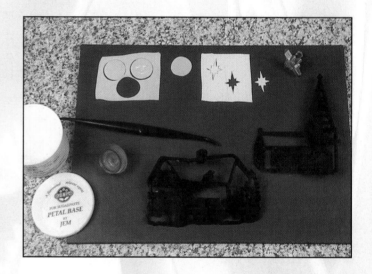

Step 5

To create the evening sky. The geranium leaf cutters found in Set L4C were cut out and positioned on the cake. A little petal dust was placed on a small piece of cotton wool and dusted onto the area representing the sky. Test the amount of dust on the cotton wool before applying to the cake surface. Remove 'leaves' to create clouds in the sky.

The Magic of Christmas

... Continued

Step 6

Holly leaves were cut out using the holly leaves found in Set A10. These were wired individually and taped into a spray. Red berries were made. A hooked taped wire was inserted into the berries. They were taped together into a little spray to fit in between the curved windows. See page 129.

Step 7

A close-up of the top of the cake.

The Magic of Christmas

This cake is dedicated to my children, Emily and Michael, to remind them of Christmas at home.

Craig's Christening Cake

A 11" (28cm) square cake has been used for this cake. The cake was placed on a 15" (38cm) cake board, and covered in white. The edge of the cake board has been covered in blue ribbon emphasising the colour scheme used in the cake. Double sided tape was used to attach the ribbon to the cake board sides.

A shell border has been piped around the cake using a No.7 star tube.

In keeping with modern trends, fairly dark colours have been chosen for this cake. Flower paste was coloured a medium blue, with a lighter blue, a maroon with a lighter maroon and a yellow. The blocks. You will need squares for the blocks. Cake could be used, cut to size, and covered in the same way as the cake, or you may prefer to use polystyrene blocks instead. It is essential that the blocks are accurately cut square. Remember polystyrene is not edible, and it should be kept out of children's reach.

Step 1

Lightly grease your worktop surface with Petal Base or white vegetable fat to prevent your flower paste from sticking to the board. Make four impressions in your flower paste with the square Cutter A, ensuring that you do not cut through the flower paste. This will give you the size of your block. Marginally reduce the size of your block so that when the sides are stuck down, the ends join neatly. Use a ruler and Tool 13 to cut around the four square impressions to give you an accurate square. You will need six sides for each block. The sides should be in a variety of colours. Allow the squares to dry.

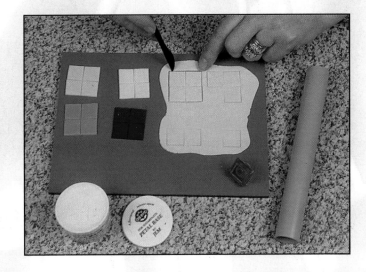

Step 2

Attach dry squares to the blocks with a little royal icing.

Craig's Christening Cake
... Continued

Step 3

When making the horse's head (J6-15) work on a Petal Pad and make an impression for the horse's eyes, using the blunt side of Tool 4A. Make the first eye on the indent made by the cutter and the next eye fairly close to it, under the second ear. Also make an impression in the ears. The same principle applies for the other animals. (Lamb - J6-10). (Dog J6-8).

Step 4

Using the sharp veining side of the same tool, you will be able to mark in the bridle across the horse's mouth and behind its ears. To add interest, you may wish to paint the animals. Petal Créme has been used on the horse.

Step 5

Numeral cutters and Alphabet Cutters were used in conjunction with animal cutters to add interest. Remember when cutting out numerals or the alphabet to work on a surface that has been lightly greased with Petal Base. Do not roll out your paste too thinly. Both the lettering and the numerals will look better if the paste is not too thin. Attach animals and lettering to blocks using a little gum glue. (Numerals Set A1) Rabbits (J6-6)

Craig's Christening Cake

... Continued

Step 6

The swan's feathers may be flat or appear to be standing up. Tool 4A could be used to flute the feathers so they appear to stand up. Outline the top of the swan's beak in black and paint the beak orange. (Swan J6-7) (Love Birds J6-5) (Blue Birds J6-9)

Step 7

To make the box on the sides of the cake, you will need the JEM Geometrical Patterns. Cutter No. A, G and J have been used. Mix two colours and then two lighter shades of each colour. The darkest shade should represent the inside of the box. Cut one using Cutter J. The lid, using Cutter G, will be the lighter shade next to the inside of the box. Using Cutter A, the square, cut the pale shade chosen for the outside of the box. Using Cutter J again, cut out the side of the box in the darker shade of the colour used for the square.

To assemble the box, place the square in position. Add the side and then the top of the box. Finally position the open lid of the box. The little duck standing on the box is taken from (Set J6-11). The little dog from set (J6-8).

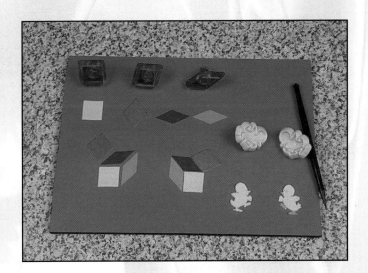

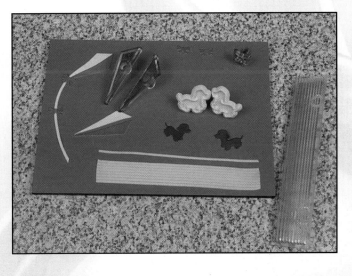

Step 8

The kite was made from E1 and E2 taken from the JEM Geometrical Patterns. The kite's tail was made from Strip No.1. The cutter for the tiny bows on the tail can be found in the JEM Miniature Wedding Set.

Craig's Christening Cake

... Continued

Step 9

Cake side detail showing box, ducks, dog and kite. Place the blocks and the desired lettering in position on the cake.

Craig's Christening Cake

This cake is dedicated to Katharine Moore, a member of the British Sugarcraft Guild, whose creative ideas using JEM products have been an inspiration to me.

Flame Lily Golden Wedding Anniversary Cake

A 9" (23cm) round cake tin was used for this cake. The cake was placed on a 13" (33cm) cake board. The cake and the board were covered simultaneously in white sugarpaste (rolled fondant). The final cake was placed on a second board that measured 16" (40cm). The cake was pushed to the back of the second board, creating a platform for the extra flowers.

Step 1

Lightly grease your worktop surface with Petal Base. Roll out white paste about 1mm thick and cut out the small doily cutter 105mm. Cut the doily exactly in half using a ruler and Tool 13A. The smallest leaf in Set A14 has been used to create a lace effect on the edge of the doily. Nine half doily pieces were required for this cake.

Step 2

A floral lace stencil JC13 was placed in the middle of each half of the doily and stencilled in with white royal icing.

HINT: Keep cutters scrupulously clean to avoid flower paste sticking in them.

Flame Lily Golden Wedding Anniversary Cake

... Continued

Step 3

Paint the little flowers and leaves with undiluted paste food colouring using a fine paint brush. Place the pieces on a 900g jam tin, or similar object, that has been covered in wax paper. Allow to dry.

Cut out more doilies in a contrasting colour. Use the small disc cutter 71mm to remove the centre, thereby creating a scalloped edge. Trim the scallops on either side to fit against the edge of the cake, at the same time, ensuring that they fit under the curve of the upright doily pieces. Using a little royal icing at the back of each side piece, attach to the cake board.

Flame Lily (Gloriosa Superba)

This flower is indigenous to Africa. It is also Zimbabwe's National flower.

Step 4

Lightly grease your worktop surface. Allowing for the insertion of taped wire gauge 26, cut out six yellow petals, using the largest water lily cutter, Set A8. Vein the petal with an orchid veiner, Set V4. Place the petal on a petal pad and lightly frill the edges with Tool 3A. Tool 4B was used to create a deep central vein in the petal. Shade the petals with orange dust on the front and the back of the petals. Insert the wire into the petal and lightly pinch the base of the petal upwards. Place the petal over a small roller to form a curve and allow to dry. The roller was secured to the board with a little Prestik. Marbles were placed on either side of the petals to allow the crease to dry correctly. Shade the base of the petals a bright green.

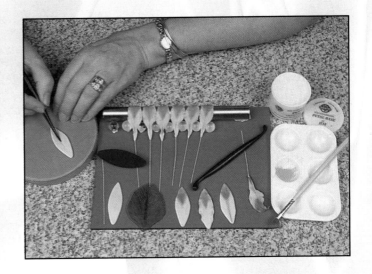

HINT: Soften the edges of petals with your fingers.

Flame Lily Golden Wedding Anniversary Cake
... Continued

Step 5

Six wire taped stamens are needed for this flower, gauge 26. The anthers should be made in green paste and should be in the shape of a tiny boat. Dip the tips of each stamen into yellow pollen. When the petals are dry, a stamen should be taped on to the base of each petal.

The pistil is made on the same gauge wire as the stamens. Tape shredded into a quarter, is used to form the three divisions that make up the stigma. Using small sharp scissors, make two incisions, creating three little tails. Hold the taped wire firmly with one hand and the tape in the other. Twist the wire. This will effectively twist the little tape ends. Neaten the ends with fingers and trim. The wire is bent at a right angle, forming a pistil that is about 1mm longer than the length of the stamens.

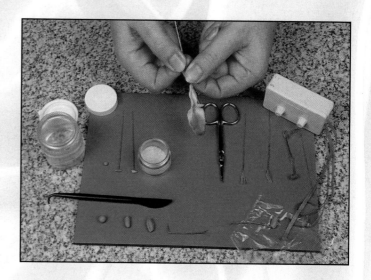

The ovary of the flower is formed with a tiny piece of green paste. This is placed on the 1cm piece of wire that will be in the middle of the flower, when the flower is fully assembled, (See Step 8). Mark in three divisions using Tool 13A. Insert the stigma into the top of the ovary whilst it is still soft. Keep this covered under clingwrap until the flower is assembled. The pistil should be below the stamens and should be facing outwards, almost at the same angle as the stamens.

Step 6

Roll out three sizes of leaves, allowing for the insertion of wire using the water lily cutters, Set A8. Vein the leaves, using the corn leaf veiners, Set V5. Roll the top of each leaf into a little sausage. Curl the tip of the leaves using a cocktail stick. Make a central vein in each leaf using Tool 4B. Dust the leaves with a bright green dust and spray with a cooking spray to give the leaves a sheen. Tape the leaves together. Tape two leaves opposite each other on the stem. Tape the next two leaves below and in between the previous leaves. Allow the smaller leaves to be at the end of the stem.

Flame Lily Golden Wedding Anniversary Cake
... Continued

Step 7

To make a bud, roll out of a ball of paste about the size of a marble. Using Tool 13A, mark in the six divisions representing the petals. Use flat tweezers to crease each division, creating the effect of petals. Insert 26 gauge wire. Tape into spray.

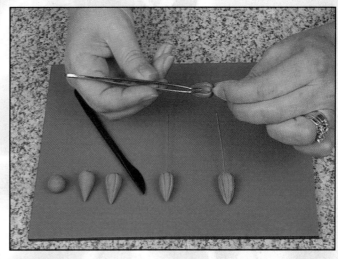

Step 8

Tape three petals together. Place the taped stem wire gauge 26 into the middle of the petals allowing 1cm of plain wire to stand above the base of the petals. (This is for the ovary and stigma.) Tape the next three petals to this. The petals will appear to be in the wrong position. Trim surplus stamen wires in layers to take away the thickness of the stem and tape securely. Using long nosed pliers, grip the stem 1cm below the petals. Bend the wire upwards through the petals, forming a 'U' hook. Carefully bend each petal downwards, creating the correct shape of the flower. Attach the ovary and stigma to the visible wire at the base of the flower at this stage.

Flame Lily Golden Wedding Anniversary Cake

Flame Lily Golden Wedding Anniversary Cake

This cake is dedicated to my dear friend, Gladiola Botha, the first National President of the South African Cake Decorators' Guild.

Recipes

TYLOSE FLOWER PASTE

Ingredients:

egg white	35ml	31g	1
sifted icing sugar	250ml	140g	1 cup
Tylose C1000p	20ml	11g	2 rounded tsp

Method:

Lightly beat egg white. Add sifted icing sugar slowly until a soft peak consistency is reached. Add the Tylose C1000p. The mixture will immediately thicken. Gradually add more sifted icing sugar until a pliable texture is achieved. Rub a little white Petal Base or white vegetable fat on your hands and work paste thoroughly. Paste should not be sticky nor should it be too hard.

Store in a sealed plastic bag in a sealed plastic container. Paste is ready to use immediately.

Note:
• If you have used an extra large egg white you may need to increase the amount of Tylose slightly.
• If the paste is too soft, you may need to work in extra sifted icing sugar.
• If the paste is too stiff, work in extra egg white.

Tylose paste has a satisfactory record of being fairly resistant to humid conditions. It is easy to make and is an economical recipe. Slightly more or less Tylose could be used to adjust the recipe to climatic conditions.

GUM GLUE, TYLOSE GLUE

Mix 5ml Tylose C1000p in 200ml water. Allow the tylose to dissolve. 5ml icing sugar may be added to this.

All the flowers in this book have been made using the Tylose recipe.

ROYAL ICING

It is recommended that a glass basin is reserved exclusively for this purpose to prevent possible contamination from any other greasy foodstuffs found in a kitchen.
All utensils used must be scrupulously clean.

1. Crack the egg white into a glass bowl. (A speck of egg yolk in this mixture will render the egg white useless).

2. Use a wooden spoon (reserved for royal icing only) or a spatula or an electric beater that has been thoroughly cleaned with boiling water to remove any possible residue of grease. Lightly beat the egg white.

3. Add sifted icing sugar one teaspoon at a time, mixing thoroughly after each addition of sugar. It is important that the sugar dissolves before adding more.

4. Continue adding sugar slowly, beating all the time. This is actually adding 'air' to the icing.

5. If you wish to use a writing tube, you will need to stop adding sugar when the soft peak consistency is reached. Soft peak means the icing will lift up into a peak with the beating utensil and will then bend over.

6. If you wish to pipe a shell border, continue adding the sieved icing sugar slowly, beating all the time until the firm peak stage is reached. This means that when you lift up the icing, the peak will remain upright.

ROYAL ICING HINTS
• Low grade stainless steel discolours royal icing.
• Hard plastic bowls retain grease.
• Soft plastic basins may splinter, causing icing nozzles to block.
• A glass basin, reserved exclusively for royal icing, is recommended.

Recipes

PASTILLAGE

Ingredients:

sieved icing sugar	500ml	280g	2 cups
water	62ml	57g	$\frac{1}{4}$ cup
gelatine	15ml	9g	3 tsp
liquid glucose	10ml	10g	2 tsp

Method:

Dissolve the gelatine in the water over a pot of hot water. Dissolve the glucose over a pot of hot water. Mix the two together. Add the icing sugar. Store in a sealed container in the fridge until required.

To use, remove only sufficient for your needs. Knead sieved icing sugar *slowly* into the mixture until it forms a paste similar to Plasticine. If the sugar is added too quickly, the paste will become coarse. Roll out on cornstarch and use immediately.:

PASTILLAGE

This is different from flower paste. Adding controlled amounts of extra sugar to a basic mixture of Pastillage will change its function. Soft pastillage could be used to pipe ornaments. Additional sugar will make it into a paste suitable for rolling out. This could be used for making plaques, cards and models. Pastillage should be rolled out on cornflour (cornstarch). It is quick drying and brittle.

SUGARPASTE

Ingredients:

icing sugar	1 kg
liquid glucose	250g
plain gelatine	10ml
white vegetable fat	20g
(not to be confused with margarine)	
solid white vegetable fat	50g

Method:

1. Stand bottle of liquid glucose (lid removed) in hot water to warm.
2. Reserve approximately 250ml icing sugar for rolling in.
3. Soak gelatine in 50ml cold water, stand in hot water until completely dissolved and clear.
4. Melt 20g fat.
5. Make a well in the sieved icing sugar, add gelatine, glucose and fat.
6. Stir well and then knead.
7. Adjust consistency by either adding icing sugar or egg white until a smooth pliable paste is obtained. Allow sugarpaste to rest for approximately two hours.
8. Knead 50g solid white vegetable fat into a small piece of sugarpaste. Knead into the remaining mixture.
9. Store in a sealed plastic bag until ready to use.

SUGAR ROCKS

Make up royal icing in the usual way using one egg white.

At peak stage, divide the mixture in two. Colour each half a different colour.

Place 1 kg of white sugar into a saucepan and just cover with water. Melt sugar slowly until the 'hard' stage is reached (this could take about 40 minutes). Keep the sides of the saucepan clean with a pastry brush, making sure no crystals form on the side of the saucepan. If this should happen, remove them with a spoon. When ready, mixture will 'tinkle' when dropped on to a glass plate.

Have a box about 12" x 12" prepared and covered with wax paper.

In a second basin, place half the royal icing. Add half of the hot syrup mixture to the first basin and stir. Mixture will bubble. Keep warm. Add the remaining half of the royal icing to the remaining syrup and stir. Combine both mixtures. Pour into the prepared box. When cool, break into rocks.

Note:

Never attempt more than this quantity at a time. The quantity may be halved.

Jem Tools

1A Small ball tool. Useful to press into blossom petals resting on foam, creating a cupped effect.

1B When using flower paste to cover sprigs and other stems which have more than one branch, this tool will help to smooth the stems.

2A A blunt ended point which may be used to begin making a trumpet shaped flower. It is also used to indent baby blossom petals resting on foam.

2B This is a fluting tool which will frill the edge of petals.

3A A very useful tool to smooth petals on the palm of your hand, or to encourage petals to curl when used on a foam surface. Use as a ball tool.

3B As for 3A, except a slightly smaller head.

4A A most useful tool for fluting and frilling petals. This tool will also help to increase the size of any petal. Its pointed tip is used to emphasize the centre of some flowers.

4B This is a veining tool, which will make vein markings difficult to create with other veiners.

5A This tool is used to form trumpet flowers.

5B The single edge of this tool may be used to make the Garrett frill. The double edge of the tool is used to mark veins on daisy petals.

6A A large ball tool for use on larger petals.

6B A shell impression which is useful to indent the edge of a plaque made out of fondant or pastillage. Also the edges of a cake board covered with fondant may be decorated using this pattern.

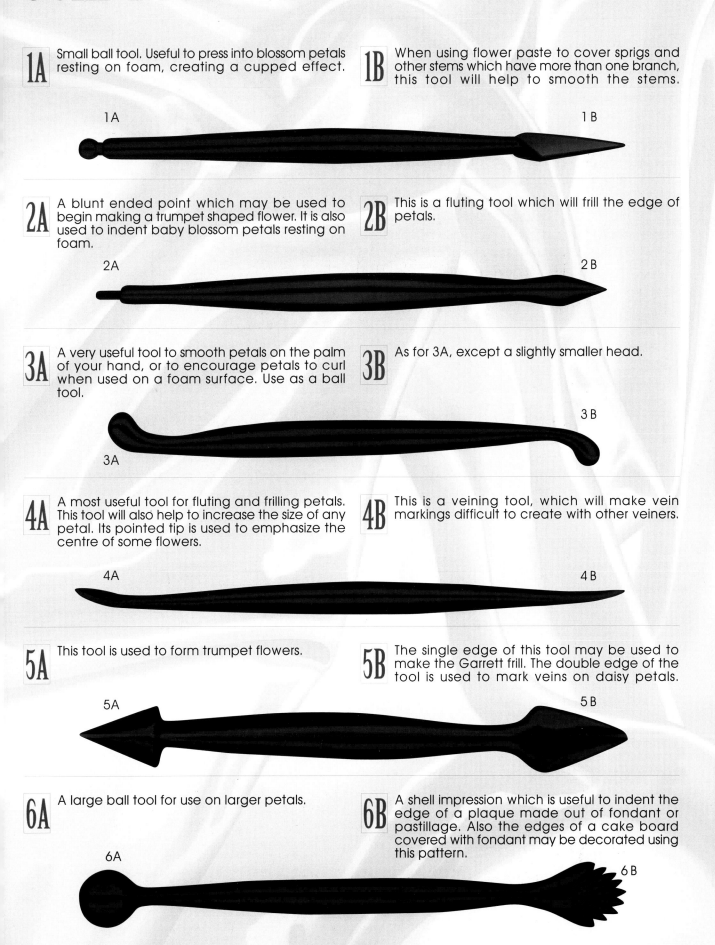

Jem Tools

7 A veining tool for a five petal trumpet flower.

8 A veining tool for trumpet flowers that have six petals.

9A Small veining tool for trumpet flowers with five petals.

9B Small veining tool for trumpet flowers with six petals.

9A   9 B

10A Small ball tool.

10B Medium ball tool.

10A   10B

11 Quilling tool. Designed especially for sugarpaste.

12A Petal veiner/friller

12B Marzipan feature tool for making 'smiles' and eyebrows.

12A   12B

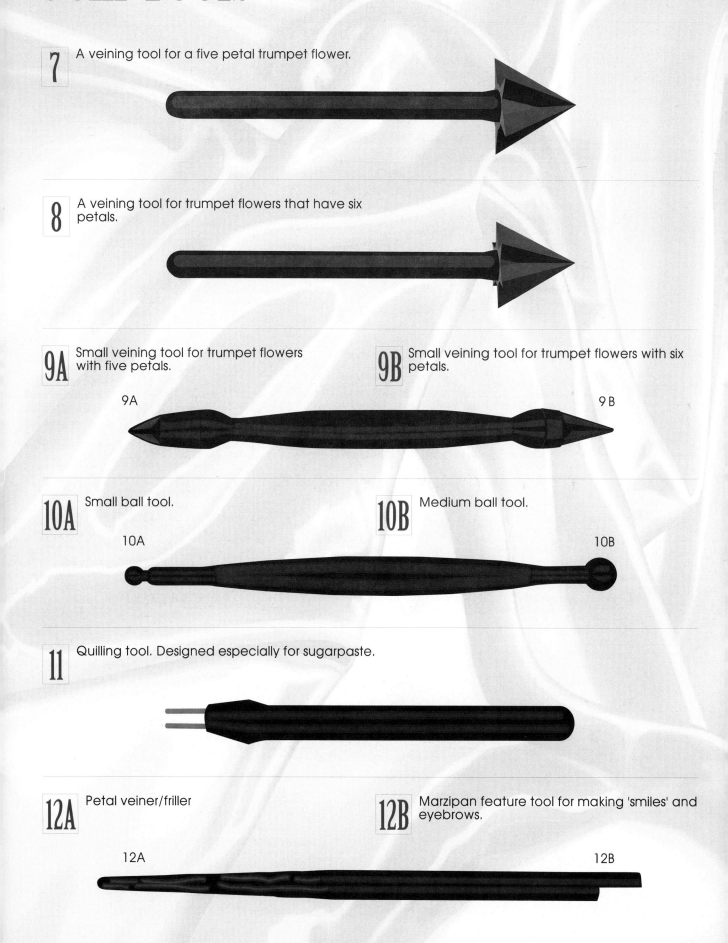

Jem Teen Tools

13A This tool has a very nice knife edge which may be used for cutting sugarpaste, or lifting up petals which have been cut out.

13B The hook may be used to grip florist tape and pull it through to the other side, when binding up a spray using florist tape.

14A Medium Friller. A ribbed frilling tool designed to be used to frill edges, as in frill cutters, or the edges of various petals.

14B Plain friller.

15A Short Friller. A very handy tool for frilling the edges of petals and the edges of cut frills. The ribbed edge is for frilling.

15B The plain side for a different effect.

16A This point is also a friller and the tip of the point may be used in the formation of small flowers.

16B Daisy point may be pressed into the centre of baby daisies causing them to 'cup'. Press flowers either on a petal pad, or a piece of sponge foam.

17 Ribbon inserter. Evenly press tool into fondant. Cut small pieces of ribbon and ease into incision.

18 Narrow Ribbon inserter

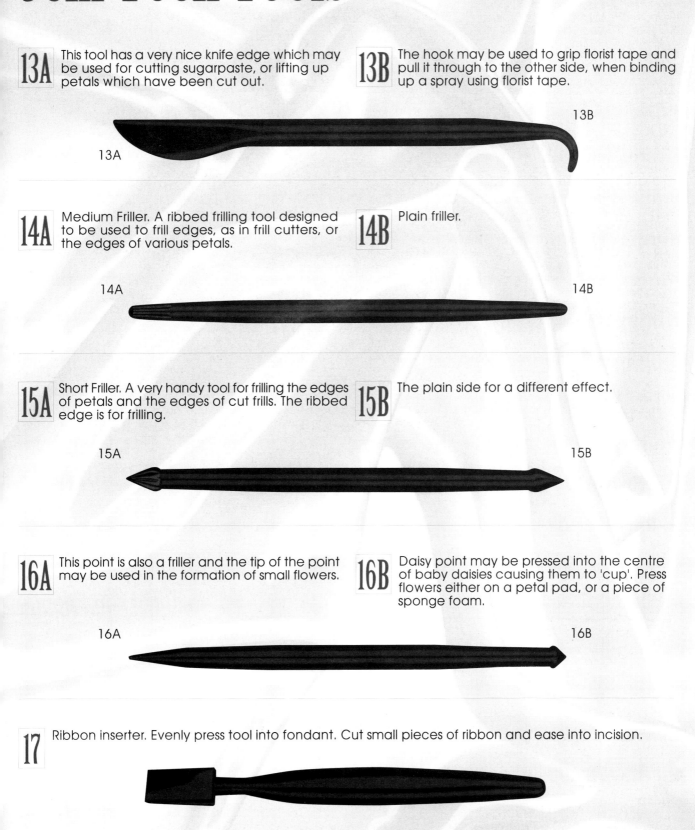

13B
13A
14A
14B
15A
15B
16A
16B

INDEX